Endorseme

This account of John Brown of Priesthill's martyrdom for his Christian beliefs over three centuries ago in rural Scotland is one that should appeal to young people the world over. Whitney Hobson Craig should be congratulated in bringing the tragic tale to life for today's reader.

DANE LOVE
Secretary, Scottish Covenanter Memorial Association,
Scotland

This is a story of courage—the kind of courage that stands for truth despite knowing there will be mortal consequences. John Brown of Priesthill was an extraordinary man whose faithful life is played out against the larger drama of the seventeenth-century conflict between England and the Scottish Covenanters. This book will inspire the reader with its intimate portrait of a man of God and at the same time, shine a light into a dark period of history.

FRANK A. JAMES, PH.D., D.PHIL.
President of Biblical Theological Seminary

This most recent biography of the Scottish Covenanter, *John Brown of Priesthill*, is the sort of story one cannot put down until it is finished! It is based on sound historical scholarship, is clearly written, and grips one's attention throughout. It is very moving and is a standing testament to the love of liberty, based on devotion to Christ and the Word of God written, that has made the blessings of Western Society possible since the death of the Scottish martyrs in the 1680s. Without the price they paid, we citizens of Great Britain and North America could never have enjoyed the freedoms that have been ours for over three hundred years. All too few of us know anything about the lives and deaths of such humble and consecrated Christians as John Brown, James Renwick, Alexander Peden and the others. Insofar as you value your liberty and the honor of Christ that is its basis, read this book to your children and grandchildren. Its lessons may be needed before the twenty-first century ends.

Douglas F. Kelly
Professor of Systematic Theology,
Reformed Theological Seminary at Charlotte

In a day of extreme historical amnesia, even among Christians, the next generation must learn of that great cloud of witnesses who testified of God's Grace without compromise, suffered for their faith, and persevered in times of trial. Among that throng of the faithful are the seventeenth-century Covenanters of Scotland, whose lives have been lost in the fog of history.

This biography encompasses the life of a devout Covenanter layman who spread the Gospel in his daily work, travelling the back roads of the Scottish lowlands selling his wares. Pursued by evil men, John Brown suffered martyrdom for his faith.

Does your son or daughter need inspiration to stand fast for Christ? The example of John Brown of Priesthill presents an unforgettable example of faithfulness, until he was murdered by government agents. His equally courageous family stood by in horror, but counted it a privilege to have had such a faithful father and husband.

Through the life of a humble layman named John Brown of Priesthill, this book introduces the next generation to great Christian men and women of the past who sacrificed everything for the glory of God.

BILL POTTER
Historian, Rockbridge Baths, Virginia

This book is set in an age of horrific terror. It touches the soul and challenges the heart. Mrs. Craig has written a compelling account of one of the great unsung heroes of liberty, John Brown. Brown's faith in his loving, sovereign God is presented with power and pathos. The author portrays the power of one individual to help bring down tyrants from their thrones. She also reveals how the movement of the Covenanters in Scotland played a central role in the elimination of religious and political tyranny throughout Europe. For those who want to know how to restore liberty in our time, this book is a must read. It will inspire and challenge those who wish to stand for Christ today by renewing their covenants (promises) to God and others.

MARSHALL FOSTER, PH.D.
Founder and President, World History Institute,
Thousand Oaks, California

Few groups in history embodied devotion, scholarship and sacrifice to our Lord more than the Scottish Covenanters. Whitney Craig masterfully tells the true story of John Brown, Covenanter martyr, whose life is full of inspiration and instruction for all followers of Christ.

KEVIN TURLEY
President, Landmark Events, Columbia, Tennessee

JOHN BROWN
of PRIESTHILL

JOHN BROWN
of PRIESTHILL

HISTORIC HEROISM IN AN ORDINARY SCOTTISH LIFE

Whitney Hobson Craig

VENTURA, CALIFORNIA

JOHN BROWN OF PRIESTHILL
Historic Heroism in an Ordinary Scottish Life
by Whitney Hobson Craig

Copyright © 2017 by Elizabeth M. Edwards

Scripture quotations are from the Geneva Bible, 1599 Edition,
Copyright © 2008 by Tolle Lege Press, LLC. Used by permission.

ISBN: 978-1-94649709-3
Library of Congress Control Number: 2017957586

Editing and Production:

Ronald W. Kirk, Editor
Diakonia Bookworks, Book Design
Cheryl Geyer, Proofreader
Michelle Shelfer, benediction.biz, Assistant Editor

Cover illustration from John Howie, *The Scots Worthies*, 2nd ed., 1879.

Printed in the United States of America.

Published by

2716 Sailor Avenue, Ventura, California 93001
1-805-642-2070 • 1-805-276-5129
NordskogPublishing.com

MEMBER

CHRISTIAN SMALL PUBLISHERS
ASSOCIATION

CONTENTS

About
ELIZABETH MCCARTY EDWARDS
Principal Sponsor & Benefactor

PUBLICATION OF THIS BOOK remembering the life of Scottish Covenanter John Brown would not be possible without the influence and generosity of Betty Edwards. Her decades-long research into the life of John Brown, her ninth great-grandfather from her grandmother Brown's side of the family, first produced a children's book called *John Brown, A Covenanter Martyr*, published in 1986. She wrote it for her grandchildren and great-grandchildren, and a host of other grandchildren and great-grandchildren of her brother and sister. Betty desired that they might rejoice over the invaluable religious privileges they enjoy due to the influence of their relative and thousands of other Covenanters in Scotland.

A life-long resident of Jackson, Mississippi, Betty has traveled the world especially enjoying visits to significant historical and Christian sites in Great Britain, Europe, Africa, South America, Asia, and the Middle East. At age 94, she continues to inspire the families of her sons, grandchildren, great-grandchildren, and others with her energy, benevolence, and love of the life-changing Good News of the Gospel. Betty is honorary vice president of the Scottish Covenanter Memorials Association of Ayrshire, Scotland.

ACKNOWLEDGMENTS

BOBBIE AMES, founder and long-time principal administrator of Emerald Mountain Christian School and the Hoffman Education Center for the Family, in Montgomery, Alabama—for her introducing this book project to Nordskog Publishing and her invaluable assistance to see *John Brown of Priesthill* published.

STEVEN EDWARDS, for invaluable assistance with correspondence representing his mother, Mrs. Betty Edwards.

FRANK A. JAMES III, D.PHIL., President and Professor of Historical Theology, Biblical Theological Seminary, Philadelphia—for historic material, counsel, and fact checking.

SAMUEL T. LOGAN, PH.D., Associate International Director, World Reformed Fellowship—for historic background.

DANE LOVE, Secretary, Scottish Covenanter Memorials Association, Ayrshire, Scotland—for historic material and fact checking.

DOTTIE PARKER, wife of Alabama State Supreme Court Justice Tom Parker—for early manuscript editing.

Foreword

by Dane Love

THE STORY OF JOHN Brown is one of the best-known tales from the time of the Covenanters in Scotland, a bloody period often referred to as the "Killing Times." Scotland was a Presbyterian country, but in 1637 King Charles tried to introduce Episcopacy as the settled form of church government, bringing it into line with England. The Scots rejected this imposition, signing a document known as the National Covenant, and thus starting a battle with authority for the next fifty years. Supporters of the National Covenant became known as Covenanters, and during the "fifty years' struggle," many were punished by fining, torture, imprisonment, banishment, and execution for their adherence to their religious beliefs.

John Brown of Priesthill was not a particularly remarkable man; in fact, he was a rather ordinary countryman, living in a remote cottage, but his Presbyterian beliefs and his devout adherence to Biblical teachings resulted in him suffering martyrdom. Hundreds of other like-minded men across Scotland suffered a similar fate, but Brown's shooting was the more noted from the fact that he was shot in front of his wife and their babe in arms. With the drowning of the Wigtown martyrs, Brown's death is one of the more celebrated stories from the time.

John Brown was probably born around 1627. He lived at Priesthill, a remote shepherd's cottage in the parish of Muirkirk, Ayrshire, Scotland, and he was known in Covenanting lore as the "Christian Carrier." In some old accounts, the name of the farm is also referred to as Priestshiel, but it is now little more than a few stones on the ground. The original Priesthill was located around one mile to the east of the present Priesthill farm, which is located amid the hills. Brown's cottage was excavated in 1926, which determined that it was of the typically old Scots long-house form, with a main living quarter and adjoining byre. A few relics are preserved in the National Museum of Scotland in Edinburgh.

John Brown was listed as a fugitive in a Royal Proclamation of 5 May 1684 for non-attendance at the curate's church. He was also wanted for harbouring Covenanters, his home being very remote. Many preachers and fugitives came to his home for shelter. It is said that Brown would have been a notable preacher but for a stammer that he suffered. However, he was often found preaching to children, and it is claimed that he was the first to run what became a "Sunday school." Brown spent many months in hiding. However, on 1 May 1685, he was working at his peat moss when a group of soldiers led by John Graham of Claverhouse came upon him. They captured him and led him back to his home. Brown's wife and young family heard the noise and came out of their home. Questions as to why Brown did not attend the church nor pray for the king were put to him, and the response was sufficient for Claverhouse to order his execution. It is said that

Brown's final prayer brought tears to the eyes of the soldiers. Claverhouse is said to have asked Isabel Brown (née Weir) if she was willing to lose her husband, to which she responded, "Heartily willing." As Brown kissed his family goodbye, Claverhouse gave the order to shoot. The soldiers stood still, refusing to carry out the command. Claverhouse is thought to have feared the soldiers were about to mutiny, so he took a pistol from his belt and shot Brown himself. Claverhouse then asked Isobel what she thought of her husband now, to which she responded, "I aye thocht muckle o' him, but never sae muckle as I do today." It has been claimed by supporters of Claverhouse, or "Bonnie Dundee" as he was known, that he did not, in fact, shoot Brown personally, but a letter written by him to the Marquis of Queensberry, which survives, records the details in his own handwriting.

John Brown was known to many notable Covenanters. The "Prophet of the Covenant," Rev Alexander Peden, regularly visited his home and it was he who carried out John and Isabel's wedding ceremony in 1682. Peden made one of his famous prophecies that day, warning Isabel that he would die within a short time.

The Societies, formed by the Covenanters when no ministers were left to lead them in prayer, also held meetings at Priesthill, one of their first meetings taking place there on 15 March 1682. An underground building was discovered at Priesthill by Claverhouse's men, big enough to hold twelve men, and within it they found swords and pistols.

The shooting of John Brown was also witnessed by his

nephew, John Browning, who had taken part in the release of Covenanter prisoners at Newmilns a few days earlier. Browning was arrested and taken to Mauchline where he was subsequently hanged. A memorial on the village green commemorates him and other martyrs executed at the same time.

At the spot where Brown was executed and buried a flat tablestone was erected, containing an epitaph that forms an acrostic—IOHN BROWNE. A later memorial was added to the side of the gravestone in 1826. John Brown's porridge bowl is preserved in the Baird Institute Museum in Cumnock, Ayrshire. The crack in the bowl being caused by a bullet is probably apocryphal!

This book has been sponsored by Betty Edwards, a long-standing supporter of the Scottish Covenanter Memorials Association. The association, a registered charity, exists to maintain the monuments to the Covenanters across Scotland and to preserve their heritage. It also wishes to ensure that the sacrifices made by the Covenanters in Scotland in the fifty years of oppression are not forgotten and to keep the story of their faith and executions alive. Many descendants of Covenanters banished to the American plantations are still aware of the Covenanting forefathers and are proud of their success in achieving the freedom to worship as one pleases, not as dictated to by authority.

It is hoped that this account of John Brown's life and execution is one that will stimulate the reader to find out more, not only about the Scottish Covenanters, but also about others whose faith has led them to suffer for the greater glory of God. That we are still interested in the life of a simple shepherd from Scotland who lived over three hundred years ago shows just how meaningful his execution was. We must be grateful that we live in civilised countries where suffering death for one's faith is no longer needed, and yet it still takes place in locations across the world.

DANE LOVE

Honorary Secretary, Scottish Covenanter Memorials Association; author of *Scottish Covenanter Stories* and *The Covenanter Encyclopaedia*

ONE

THE COVENANTERS

JOHN BROWN OF PRIESTHILL was a Covenanter. What is a Scottish Covenanter? Firstly, he is Scottish. Scotland is the northern part of the Island of Great Britain on the west coast of the European continent, where it is subject to the harsh climate of the North Atlantic and the North Sea. The rugged land of Scotland does not yield easily and neither do the Scots who live upon it.[1]

Secondly, simply put, the Scottish Covenanters were earnest and devout, Biblically minded Christians—Presbyterians—who recognized no other Lord than Jesus Christ. The notion of covenant in the historic Christian church derives from the Biblical Old Testament agreements, by which for example the people of the nation of Israel committed themselves to their God. Scotland, led by John Knox, originally declared itself a Presbyterian nation in 1560. Later in the face of the growing power of their English neighbors to the south, two central covenantal declarations in Scottish history—first the *National Covenant* and later the *Solemn League and Covenant*—gave the Covenanters their name and identity. As Abraham made his commitment to God by covenant, the

---

1. We recommend to the earnest student a rich though idealized portrait of the Scottish people and their history in the stories and poems of Scottish authors Sir Walter Scott and Robert Louis Stevenson.

Scots covenanted with God to uphold Presbyterian polity. For many, it became a matter of life and death. Giving one's life out of love for and to defend the Gospel foundation of one's country is the essence of patriotism.

Many Scots in 1638 personally signed the *National Covenant* to uphold the Presbyterian religion. Again in 1643, they signed the *Solemn League and Covenant*, a treaty with the English Parliamentarians to preserve Scotland's Presbyterian heritage. The English Civil War (1642–1651) pitted Calvinistic Puritans against Royalists. The Puritans shared the Covenanter love of liberty. The Royalists believed in a more or less absolute authority of the king. At first the Puritans prevailed, but the Royalists eventually overpowered the Puritan parliament. With this change, the Scottish Covenanters became vulnerable to the imperial, established English religion of Anglicanism.[2] The Scots took a stand for religious liberty, which led to half a century of persecution (1638–1689). This persecution led eventually to widespread migration to Ulster in Ireland and the American colonies, yet many remained in Scotland. At the heart of the Scottish Covenanters movement was the deep-seated conviction that there was but one Head of the Kirk—the Scottish term for *church*—Jesus Christ. The Covenanters refused to accept a temporal King in that role.

---

2. Anglicanism resulted from King Henry VIII's split with the Roman Catholic Church beginning in 1532. While considered Reformed as the Covenanters were, the Anglican Church retained many elements of state authority inherent in Romanism.

This opposition to the king gave rise to all their troubles.

The Scottish poet preacher George Gilfillan offers a vivid personal description of the Scottish Covenanters:

> They were terribly in earnest. The passion that was in them, like all great passions, refused to be divided. Their idea possessed them with a force and a fullness to which we find few parallels in history. It haunted their sleep, it awoke with them in the morning—it walked, like their shadow, with them to business or to pleasure—it became the breath of their nostrils and the soul of their soul.[3]

The Scottish Covenanter movement lasted from 1637 to 1690. During this time, historians estimate that the government banished a total 1,700 people to work on plantations in the Americas, 750 to the Northern Islands, while they imprisoned 3,600. Seven thousand fled to other countries; 498 were murdered; 362 died by execution (often merely murdered under legal authority); and 680 died of wounds, often the result of warfare.[4]

The Covenanters believed their faith to be dearer than their very lives. Many Covenanters died as martyrs, not the least of whom was John Brown, the Christian Carrier of Priesthill.

---

3. George Gilfillan, *The Martyrs, Heroes and Bards of the Scottish Covenant* (London: Cockshaw, 1852), 88–90.

4. John Howie and W. H. Carslaw, *The Scots Worthies* (Edinburgh: Banner of Truth Trust, 1995), 442–445.

TWO

EARLY LIFE

CONTRARY TO POPULAR MOVIES and fictional literature, most heroes do not stand out in history. Their quiet courage in a just cause leaves behind an inspiring legacy. However obscure, we must view them as heroes. John Brown of Priesthill, a humble commoner in an age of often arbitrary aristocratic authority, is one of these.

As with most individuals and events of the 1600s, very few records testify to the life of John Brown of Priesthill. His gravestone places his birth in the year 1627. In that year, the son of King James I—the future Scottish and English King—Charles I had begun his scheming against the Scottish Presbyterians.

As with many others living ordinary lives on the land with no extraordinary accomplishments to recount, we lack details of the man John Brown. Yet from other writings of the time, we may compose an imaginative but fairly accurate portrait of the young John Brown's family life.

Young John Brown knew no noble life of wealth and leisure, but grew up in humble surroundings. All historical records place John living near the village of Muirkirk, Ayrshire, Scotland, a hamlet some distance south of the closest city of Glasgow. It is reasonable to conclude that he lived there for most, if not all, of his life. At that time in Scotland, a common person would not move around very much, but would stay close to the family's hometown.

In the earliest known record, a charter of the Monks of Melrose described Muirkirk in 1176 as a roaming forest filled with wild animals. Unfortunately, pioneering settlers thoughtlessly and to little purpose chopped down those trees. The mass of the many, decaying fallen trees caused a suffocation of the soil resulting in an abundance of moss, but a dearth of leafing plants. The remaining boggy land could then best produce peat, used as a heating fuel, but little other useful vegetation. Few resources in this place suggest a hard life for those who dwelt there.

The village of Muirkirk grew about the new parish church, which broke away from Mauchline in 1631, with the Reverend John Reid as minister. The kirk session of elected ruling elders went about establishing many standards for their parishioners. The elders held everyone to a strict code of conduct. They supervised morals, forbade drunkenness, required church attendance and enforced Sabbath observance. Community life centered around the church.

Church services followed an orderly form like most contemporary Presbyterian churches. They opened with prayer, confessed sins in a silent prayer, sang the *Gloria Patri*, listened to a sermon, and took communion at the Lord's Table. The officiating minister finished with a benediction, praying the blessings of God on His people. The various parts of the *liturgy* may have occurred at different times within the services, but they practiced all these elements in worship.

At that time, the common people generally ate oatmeal as their common grain. Breads, cakes, porridge, and soups utilized oatmeal. They also ate whatever vegetables they could grow themselves and the meats they could trap or hunt. Farmers paid rent to their landlords with half of their production. This meant in years of poor harvest that families could face starvation. They made clothing from rough wool. Many went barefoot year-round.

In 1643, 145 people between the ages of sixteen and sixty resided in the Muirkirk area. No school then existed and apparently no one made an effort to build one. As a result, families provided for most learning within the home.

When reading about the Covenanters, the American Pilgrims, or any staunchly religious people, do we with difficulty imagine them as anything but doleful and always at their prayers? However, like the Pilgrims, the Covenanters loved life. They laughed, cried and conversed just like anyone else. They simply valued the freedom of religion and would fight for it.

The Covenanters greatly enjoyed singing. Many existing accounts indicate that they would often gather and spend time singing the Psalms and popular tunes of the day. Some accounts suggest they enjoyed group folk dancing. They commonly engaged in laughter and joking.

They also placed great emphasis on humanitarianism. They took care of the poor and sick. They tended to widows and provided homes to orphaned children. While few had money, none hesitated to give what they had to anyone in sincere need. While the Covenanters knew how to have fun, they lived as a moral people with firm standards and high expectations. As a result, peer pressure kept them accountable to one another.

John Brown's farm, known as Priesthill (pronounced *preeshle*), lay secluded in the wilderness of Ayrshire, nearly four miles from nearby Muirkirk. It sat in a small valley on the side of a hill, estimated to be about 1100 feet above sea level. Quiet rolling hills and moorland surrounded. Perhaps not entirely accurately, yet oft repeated, the saying goes that on a clear day you can see as far as Pentland (behind Edinburgh) to the east, Goat Fell to the west, the Bens of the Northern Highlands, and the Galloway hills to the south. Actually, one may discover these views from the hilltops surrounding Priesthill. With the River Ayr's source lying nearby, the Browns could hear its contributing streams gurgling and rippling throughout the area. The thoughtful reader might imagine Priesthill as a place of quiet repose and pleasant industriousness.

Some records indicate that John had a rebellious youth and cared little for religion. Eventually, as an adult, he converted to follow Christ. By this time, due to increasing persecution, many began to abandon the regular churches and meet secretly among the glens and hills in *conventicles*. Conventicles are meetings, and as the Covenanters used the term, *dissenting* religious gatherings. Despite the persecution, the Covenanter movement grew quickly. Many came to know Christ through these meetings and left renewed in their faith. John could have been one of these men. Later in life, he developed a close friendship with Alexander Peden, a popular Covenanter minister. John may have come to Christ during one of Peden's sermons. Peden later became a mentor to John.

John Brown married Janet Ritchart sometime in the 1640s. While some sources claim the couple had two sons, we cannot truly know much about this marriage and family. John and Janet cked out a living at their farm and, by all accounts, lived a happy and peaceful life together. Unfortunately, Janet died in 1678, the same year their daughter Janet was born. That mother Janet was then nearly fifty years old suggests she died from complications of childbirth. John must have then faced rearing a newborn alone. What immense grief and struggles he must have felt.

Janet's will survives to this day. In it, she left John twenty sheep, one cow, a *stirk* (heifer) and an old *meir* (mare). Janet also left behind significant debt—two years rent to "Loudoun" (the Earl of Loudoun), a loan from a relative, a debt to the minister, one fee to a lass, and another to the *herd laddie* John Brouning.

Undoubtedly, this time brought financial hardship and emotional distress. In the face of everything happening around him, imagine how John felt and what strength he needed to care for his little girl. Yet a man of God knows to Whom to turn.

THREE

THE CHRISTIAN CARRIER

MONEY DID NOT YET generally circulate among the common people. Most turned instead to trade and barter arrangements. Many farmed and sourced their own food, as well as weaving and sewing clothing and other fabric needs. During this epoch of history, people generally remained self-sufficient. When in need of additional supplies, they would barter their own homemade items or leftover produce when in need of additional supplies.

The need for barter meant the need to travel some distance. However, in Scotland in the 1600s, the roads were rough at best and often did not exist at all. The hilly terrain, rocky and uncertain, made it difficult for carriages to travel effectively. Oftentimes instead, someone from the community would, utilizing a push cart or pack horse, hike into the surrounding areas to trade for necessary items.

John Brown accepted this responsibility as a *carrier* to support his family. No record reveals how long he maintained this enterprise. Acting as a humble carrier could not better John's social standing, but it does illustrate a certain courage, wise bartering skill, honesty, and reliability. His neighbors *trusted* him to travel away with their valuables seeking the things they needed. In return, he brought back the desired goods he bargained in trade.

As John travelled plying his trade, he heard the latest news regarding the Scottish government and church. As such, he became the primary source of news for his community. His occupation most likely played a large part in his becoming a leading Covenanter. He often found himself speaking with other Covenanters, and then participating in the establishment of their secret denomination. Likely, John spread the news regarding planned conventicles and the needs of suffering fellow Covenanters.

As a result of his trade and consequent Covenanter activity, his neighbors came to call John Brown the "Christian Carrier of Priesthill." Again, as his occupation suggests, he must have demonstrated great trustworthiness and honesty, above reproach in his dealings material and spiritual. His honorific title also highlights his commitment to and enthusiasm for the faith of Christ.

In 1637, King Charles I of England and Scotland imposed his *Book of Canons* on the Scots and required Scottish authorities to enforce it, with punishment for refusal. As the situation grew dire and dangerous for devout Covenanters in Scotland due to the imperious suppression of religious freedom by the king, John often found himself passing unpleasant news along to his fellow Covenanters in the community.

In 1662, Charles assembled a Privy Council in Glasgow.[1] History knows this Council as the "Drunken Parliament."

---

1. *Privy* essentially means *private*. Here it particularly means a group of elite special counselors to the ruler or rulers.

In this questionable condition—its decision-making capabilities greatly impaired—the Privy Council handed down on May 8, 1662, a proclamation outlawing any religious meeting not adhering to the Anglican *Book of Common Prayer*. John Brown must share the news that this tyrannical organ of the English state made any other religious gathering strictly illegal to lead or attend. The king charged the military with responsibility to carry out this law by collecting fines and enforcing Anglican church attendance. This proclamation further demanded that all who held public office must declare an oath of allegiance to the government and its established church. Covenanters found themselves unwelcome and criminalized for their beliefs.

In 1666, John would have again relayed troubling news to his fellow Covenanters. Angered at ill treatment, deception, and the unjust deaths of fellow believers, a large group of Covenanters armed themselves in self-defense. They managed to capture James Turner, the leader of the government troops assigned to enforce the anti-Covenanter laws. Turner's capture emboldened them in their high excitement to attack Edinburgh. This would demonstrate their resolve not to accept religious slavery. However, many soon realized they could not win a battle and decided to return home. The remaining small force of about 900 men, with no military experience or skill, and very little in the way of weaponry, arrived in the Pentland Hills where they took some rest. Abandoning the intent to engage the government forces in battle, they decided peacefully to plead their case to the Privy

Council in Edinburgh. However, a royal army of 3,000 dragoons attacked them—mercilessly killing many. The survivors faced ultimate punishment. Convicted as traitors, they must die.

Ill will toward Covenanters continued to grow. The established government—the Scots Estates—would use this incident, known as Pentland Rising, as a political weapon against the Covenanters throughout the entire ensuing long battle for religious liberty.

In 1674, John carried the sad tidings that the Scots Estates strengthened the laws against Covenanters by declaring anyone caught attending or participating in a conventicle must die by execution and all property confiscated. The Estates promised monetary reward to those who divulged the locations of conventicles and the identities of attending persons. To soften the blow of these laws and further entire submission, the Estates also passed an Act of Indemnity. Under this law, to escape punishment for their "past crimes," Covenanters could recant and surrender to the authorities. Few submitted to this new act.

To further gain Covenanter obedience and submission, the Estates used the carrot and the stick. They both enforced obligations and restrictions, while simultaneously offering incentives. For example, the government forced Covenanter families in the south to host over 6,000 Highlanders for three months in 1678. *Highlanders* are the historic people and culture of the mountainous portions of Scotland, generally in the north and west. These mountains range generally from about 2,500 feet elevation to over 4,000. The mostly Gaelic—historic Scottish—people of the Highlands are known for their toughness, much due to the harshness of the land, and for the long heritage of their unique way of life and culture, the result of relative isolation. In contrast, the Lowlanders live among the lower, mostly hilly elevations. Due to accessibility and proximity to England, the Lowlands culture reflects more of the English and European influence.

During this time of government coercion, the government gave the Highlanders free reins to plunder, terrorize, and abuse the Covenanters. "They robbed them of their propriety (property)."[2] This plan backfired on the government as the Highlanders soon did not bother to distinguish between the Covenanters and "loyal subjects." The Highlanders merely terrorized everyone. In the shame of their poor judgment, the government recanted and ordered the Highlanders to return to their homes. Many of them left with their horses piled so high with plunder that one man describes them as if they had "been at the sack of a besieged city."[3] John Brown and his young daughter most likely *hosted* a few Highlanders in this time of grief.

Not all was all gloom and doom as John carried out his work and circulated the news of Scotland. Eventually, in the sum-

---

2. Hector Macpherson, *Scotland's Battles for Spiritual Independence* (Edinburgh: Oliver & Boyd, 1905), 118.

3. John Beveridge, *The Covenanters* (Edinburgh: T. & T. Clark, 1905), 55–83.

mer of 1678, the Covenanters responded to a fresh onslaught of persecution by hosting the largest conventicle on record at Skeoch Hill in the Lowlands parish of Irongray in Dumfriesshire on the southern edge of Scotland. According to one of the ministers who led this conventicle, John Welsh, about 6,000 people attended. He recalled that the order of worship began with everyone singing the 121st psalm. They spent three hours each in the opening and closing ceremonies. In between, Communion required over eight hours so that everyone might participate. They considered Communion essential, but it had become rare as the government banned formal gathering. Therefore, such an important act, one established by Jesus Christ Himself, sadly became a rare occurrence for the Covenanters. As such, they eagerly sought out opportunities to partake in the Communion sacrament with ordained ministers. Providentially and no doubt with great gratitude, the Covenanters escaped ambush and worshipped in peace that day.

The ordinary demands of life quite filled John's time. He worked his farm and exercised his important responsibilities as the carrier, of course, but he also made time to study his Bible. Most likely, John had learned from Covenanter ministers with seminary degrees. He expressed a considerable wealth of knowledge about faith and the Bible. Originally, with such a solid understanding of Scriptures, his teachers thought him an ideal candidate for the ministry. However, from birth, John struggled with a considerable stutter. Many accounts confirm a difficulty in ordinary conversation due to his speech impediment.

However, John possessed a powerful gift of spiritual spoken prayer. He knew how to approach God and converse easily with him. When John prayed, his stutter disappeared. He spoke clearly with strength and conviction at the throne of God. However, when his prayers ended, his stutter returned. Due to his handicap, he could not successfully enter the ministry. Presumably, a stuttering pastor would soon frustrate parishioners.

Yet despite his stutter, he remained eager to teach and share the Word of God. Curiously, John Brown's literate learning was unusual among carriers and among the rural populace in general. In Scotland as in most places in Europe, a large gap in learning existed between the common laboring class and the educated ruling class. The answer lies in the Protestant Biblical faith. The educational gap began to narrow with the advent of the Reformation. The goals of the Reformation—godly living in Christ—required personal Biblical knowledge, which required the ability to read and reason. At least as far back as early reformer John Wycliffe, and certainly from the times of Martin Luther, John Calvin, and John Knox, the value of a literate education began to flourish among Protestant Christians. As the Covenanters, so the American Pilgrims and Puritans strongly believed in education. That love and value of learning greatly contributed to America's liberty and prosperity, to which the Covenanter emigrants to America would contribute. Biblical literate education is key to the establishment and maintenance of Christian liberty and justice.

In this spirit of godly learning, John founded what we would recognize today as a *Sunday School*. The ruling Scots Estates either banished or killed many Covenanting men for their faith, leaving behind children without fathers or manly leadership to instill a Biblical faith in them. John recognized this need. He opened his home every Monday night to young people with a hunger for Biblical learning. Students would walk miles across the difficult terrain to avail themselves of John's teaching and guidance. For textbooks, he used the Bible and the *Westminster Confession of Faith*. In the summer, everyone would gather outside in the sunshine to study and pray. In the winter, they would go to his home, where they would gather in a large circle around the fire. All the while, the group exercised great caution since such a gathering (by definition a conventicle) would bring the same punishment as preaching—death for the participants.

More than likely, the study followed Walter Smith's "Twenty-Two Steps of Defection" and "Rules for Society Meetings."[4] For an idea of how John's teaching sounded and the orderliness expected, consider this passage from "Rules for Society Meetings":

> As it is the undoubted duty of all to pray for the coming of Christ's kingdom, so all that love our Lord Jesus Christ in sincerity, and know what it is to bow a knee

---

4. Patrick Walker, *Biographia Presbyteriana Vol. II, Containing the Lives of the Rev. Mr. Donald Cargill, and Mr. Walter Smith* (Edinburgh: D. Speare and J. Stevenson, 1927), 62–88.

in good earnest, will long and pray for the out-making of the gospel promises to His Church in the latter days, that King Christ would go out upon the white horse of the gospel, conquering and to conquer, and make a conquest of the travail of His soul, that it may be sounded that the kingdoms of the world are become His, and His Name called upon from the rising of the sun to its going down.

That the old casten (weighty ways) of Israel would never be forgotten, especially in these meetings. That the promised day of their ingrafting might be hastened; and that dead weight of blood removed off them, that their fathers took upon them and upon their children, that have sunk them down to hell, upwards of seventeen hundred years.

That the Lord's written and preached word may be sent with power to enlighten the poor Pagan world, living in black perishing darkness without Christ and the knowledge of His Name . . . that they would love, sympathise, and pray for one another in secret, and in their families who have them, and weep when any member weeps, and rejoice with all such as are joined in this society communion which is the strictest of all communions; and before they go to their meetings everyone would be importunate with the Lord to go with them and meet with them, that it may be for the better and not for the worse, and with all such meetings.[5]

---

5. Walter Smith, *A Directory Or, Rules and Directions for Fellowship-*

The formal institution of Sunday School came almost a century later when Robert Raikes of Gloucester made it his calling to minister to the English children of the Industrial Revolution, children who otherwise received little to no literate education.[6] But John Brown should qualify as a forerunner in the godly education of needy children.

---

meetings *Their Mutual Edification and Uniformity. By the Pious and Worthy Mr. Walter Smity Martyr for the Truth under the Late Tyranny. To Which Is Added, the Reverend Mr. John Hepburn's Rules for Fellow-meetings* (Belfast: William Murdoch, Chapman, 1753).

6. See for example, Albert Gregory, *Robert Raikes, Journalist and Philanthropist: A History of the Origin of Sunday Schools* (London: Hodder and Stoughton, 1877).

FOUR

FRIENDSHIP WITH AULD SANDY

JOHN BROWN FOSTERED FRIENDSHIPS with many Covenanters. One of his closest friends was a minister named Alexander Peden. Many believe that Peden witnessed Jesus Christ to John and played a key role in his salvation. He famously described John Brown as "a clear shining light, the greatest Christian I ever conversed with." Peden, often referred to as Auld (old) Sandy, held a reputation as a dramatic and eccentric character.

Alexander Peden was born several miles west of Muirkirk in Sorn, Ayrshire, in 1626. His father tended a small property, likely as tenant of the Earl of Loudoun, and left Alexander a fair patrimony when he died. This gave Peden an entryway into Scottish high society. However, he knew in his heart that God called him to the ministry. At age 23, he bought a Bible and inscribed in it, "Alexander Pedine, My Own Hand, AET. 23 Years, 1649." This worn and well-used Bible survives to this day and bears witness to his ministry.

For a short time, Peden taught school and acted as a song leader and session clerk for Rev. John Guthrie of Tarbolton. He then attended seminary at Glasgow University and began his ministry at New Luce in Galloway, south west Scotland, in 1659 at the age of 33. Eyewitnesses describe him as being tall and handsome with a peculiar fervor in preaching.

In 1662, as part of the Drunken Parliament's legislation, Charles received supreme spiritual authority within Scotland and could appoint bishops to enforce his standards. According to the statutes, all pastors must submit to the government and preach from the Episcopalian liturgy. If they refused, they forfeited three months of compensation, lost both their church ministry and their home in the church manse. Dissenting preachers could not preach anywhere within 25 miles of their previous pastorate or *curate*. The government then replaced many ministers with those who agreed with the government's church ordinances. Well trained Anglican candidates were rare, resulting in a Biblically and literately ignorant church ministry. Many were nothing but rude, opportunistic herdsmen who leapt at the chance of making a good living, though they could provide little good teaching to the congregation, even if they were inclined to give it.

As a result, parishioners stopped gathering for church. Instead, they attended the secret conventicles, frequently led by their former pastors. The churches slowly grew empty, which angered the Scottish Privy Council. Seeking to regain control of the church, the Council made attendance mandatory with membership rolls posted on the doors of the church to expose those who did not show up. The Council fined absentees or evicted them from their homes. Some received beatings for their *crimes*.

On November 1, 1662, four hundred ministers left their parishes in Scotland. Peden joined these ranks. On Peden's last Sunday in his kirk, he preached over twelve hours, with his parishioners crying and hanging on every word. When Peden finished preaching, he went to the church door and knocked three times and declared in a loud voice: "In my master's name, I arrest thee! That none enter thee but as I have done—by the door," a reference to Jesus' words in John 10. This act was Peden's way of dramatizing the fundamental commitment of congregation to the authority of the Bible and its faithful preaching. Amazingly enough, no one else preached in that church throughout the duration of the Covenanter struggle.

Peden had been part of the Pentland Rising struggle and so became a wanted man. Unable to catch him, the Privy Council began to pin various *crimes* on him—preaching at conventicles, baptizing children, and presiding over the Lord's Supper. Congregants risked much, really everything, to congregate. By this time, the Council criminalized even speaking to or feeding a Covenanter.

Aware that the authorities continually pursued him and to spare families from danger of the authorities, Peden would not board with families in their homes. Instead, he began to live life as a wandering preacher. He preached during the day and slept outdoors at night. Local legend says that he knew all the caves in the southern region of Scotland. He often made his home in them and stayed in one or the other for long stretches of time, claiming it as his own. This knowledge of the caves would be helpful over the years when the caves would provide several often narrow escapes from the authorities.

The Council officially posted a charge against him in January 1666:

> The said Mr. Alexander Peden did keep a Conventicle at Ralston, in the parish of Kilmarnock, about the 10th of October last, where he baptized the children of Adam Dickie, Robert Lymburner, and many others; as also he kept a Conventicle at Craigie parish, at the Castle-Hill, where he baptized the children of William Gilmor in Kilmarnock, and Gabriel Simpson, both in the said parish, and that besides twenty-three children more; both which Conventicles were kept under cloud of night, with a great deal of confusion, as also the said Mr. Alexander rides up and down the country with sword and pistol, in grey clothes.[1]

He had several close calls as he hid in the hills. One of the most remarkable incidences occurred when Peden led a conventicle in Auchengreoch. He had barely escaped capture a few days before, and the soldiers thought he had fled the area. As Peden preached at the conventicle, dragoons suddenly surrounded the crowd. The crowd, filled with fear, turned to Peden for advice. Peden prayed as they discussed possible ways to escape:

> Lord, we are ever needing at Thy hand, and if we had not Thy command to call upon Thee in the day of trou-

---

1. Thomas Cameron, *Peden the Prophet: "Puir Auld Sandy"* (Edinburgh: Blue Banner Productions, 1998), 27–30.

ble, and Thy promise of answering us in the day of our distress, we wot not what would become of us. If Thou have any more work for us in Thy world, twine them about the hill, Lord, and cast the lap of Thy cloak over poor old Sandy and these people, and we will keep it in remembrance, and tell it to the commendation of thy goodness, piety, and compassion, what Thou didst for us at such a time.[2]

As he finished praying, a thick fog suddenly descended upon the crowd. The mounted soldiers could not see gathering at all, and Peden escaped. The people no doubt thanked God for this deliverance. But also from this day, fellow Covenanters revered Peden as a prophet.

In July of 1669, the Scottish government offered a pardon or indulgence to the ministers if they would promise complete submission authorities. Only forty ministers accepted. Immediately they regained a life of peace, but at the expense of slavish submission to the king's authority. Again in 1672, the government offered an indulgence. Eighty ministers accepted and surrendered. Then came the 1674 Act of Indemnity, at about the same time that preaching at a conventicle became a capital crime. Those who accepted these pardons found the Covenanter life too difficult and desired to return to the comfort of the mainstream. This reminds us of Jesus' words: "[H]e that taketh not his cross, and followeth after

---

2. J. Meldrum Dryerre, *Heroes and Heroines of the Scottish Covenanters* (London: S.W. Partridge, 1896).

me, is not worthy of me. He that will find his life, shall lose it; and he that loseth his life for my sake, shall find it" (Matt. 10:38–39, 1599 Geneva Version).

Accepting an indulgence became a complex choice. On one hand, government, society, and the state church would no longer treat submitters as criminals. On the other hand, their Covenanter friends would view them as traitors and cowards. These indulgences caused much strife and in-fighting among the brethren, a great evil in itself.

Never one to comfort himself in the mainstream, Peden continued to preach at conventicles. After years of exposure to the elements and living in the wilderness, Peden made his way to Ireland for refuge. However, Ireland suffered royal religious persecution like that in Scotland. Shortly after his arrival there, Irish authorities captured him when they intercepted a letter from Peden to a friend. Authorities returned him to Edinburgh for sentencing in the summer of 1673. Relishing the opportunity finally to punish Peden, the Council sent him to Bass Rock, a miserable prison located on a rocky island and designed solely for the punishment of Covenanters. While there, Peden sent the following letter to friends:

> We are close shut up in our chambers; not permitted to converse, diet, or worship together; but conducted out by two at once in the day, to breathe in the open air— envying the birds their freedom, provoking and calling on us to bless Him for the most common mercies. Again, we are close shut up day and night to hear only

the sighs and groans of our fellow prisoners. O for grace to credit Christ, hitherto never cumbersome, and His Cross in whatever piece of service, in bonds or freedom, He cuts out! I return to thank you for your seasonable supply, money and contributions, an evidence of your love to Him and your affectionate remembrance of us. Persuade yourself you are in our remembrance, though not so deep as we in yours, yet making mention of you to your and our Master, begging you may be directed, supported and carried through cleanly in this our hour of temptation; acquitting yourselves as watchmen from your watch-tower, fulfilling your ministry which you have received from the Lord. So prayeth your unworthy and affectionate well-wisher in bonds.—Alexander Peden.[3]

After five hard years imprisoned at Bass Rock, the Scottish government banished Peden to America. He reacted by prophesying to his fellow prisoners that *"the ship has not been built that would bear them over the sea to any of the plantations."*[4] Events soon proved him correct when the boat docked in London. There all the prisoners went free.

For the next five years, Peden divided his time between Scotland and Ireland, secretly preaching in the countryside in one or the other place. As it turned out, he often received refuge in the hospitality of John Brown of Priesthill.

---

3. Dryerre, *Heroes and Heroines of the Scottish Covenanters.*
4. Ibid.

FIVE

A COVENANTED MARRIAGE

AFTER THE DEATH OF his wife, John continued to work as a carrier to support his little daughter, Janet. This was a time of struggle and sorrow as John tried to fill the shoes of two parents to a very young girl. When John came home, students filled their house. Home seemed safe and warm with the fellowship of God. Father and daughter undoubtedly grew closer through the love and sorrow shared within.

Sometime in 1680, John became friends with the Weir family in Sorn, Alexander Peden's home parish. As a carrier, John frequently dealt with Mr. Weir and soon found that they shared Covenanter convictions. As John grew closer to Mr. Weir, he also grew to know his family. Mr. Weir had a daughter, Isabel,[1] a woman imbued with a cheerful spirit and humorous disposition. With her additional strong faith and good morals, before long John found himself falling in love with her.

John must have been several years older than Isabel, perhaps by 20 or more years. Nonetheless, she soon fell in love with him as well. With her cheerful but strong spirit, she was a good match for John Brown. John and Isabel's mutual sympathy grew over their two-year-long courtship.

---

1. Sometimes spelled *Isobel.*

At some point during their courtship, John told Isabel of a premonition. He must one day die for his faith. As he proposed to her, he asked her if she would be supportive of him, defending his faith even in death. She responded, "If it should be so, through affliction and death I will be your comfort. The Lord has promised me grace and he will give you glory."[2] They began to plan a wedding. John announced the good news to John and Isabel's good friend and confidant Sandy Peden, busy baptizing children across Kyle. He could not resist. And in April of 1682, Sandy officiated the marriage ceremony in a glen near Priesthill.

At first, they intended that the wedding should be a small, quiet affair—just the two of them and their immediate family. However, when Isabel arrived at the ceremony, she found a large crowd of friends and family gathered to witness their vows. Disturbed by the sight, Isabel worried that the great gathering risked discovery by the dragoons roaming the country.

According to William McGavin, Peden calmed her thoughts by saying, "They are all friends, and have come at the risk of their lives to hear God's word, and to countenance his ordinance of marriage."[3] The wedding was a true conventicle, with singing, worship and celebratory fellowship of believers.

---

2. William McGavin, *Memoirs of John Brown, of Priesthill, and the Rev. Hugh Mackail, Two Sufferers for the Cause of the Covenanted Reformation in Scotland* (n.p., 1839), 31–36.

3. Ibid.

Isabel and John rejoiced in the presence of such loving witnesses of their new marriage union. Upon completing the ceremony, Peden took Isabel aside with one of his prophetic insights. He said, "You have a good man to be your husband—value him highly; keep linen beside you to be your winding-sheet; for in a day when you least expect it thy master will be taken from your head. In him the image of our Lord and Saviour is too visible to go unnoticed by those who drive the chariot wheels of persecution through the breadth and length of bleeding Scotland. But fear not, thou shalt be comforted."[4]

Peden's words never drifted far from Isabel's thoughts. In her days of joyful married life with John, she could not shed an ever-present sense of foreboding. She deeply believed that someday they must face extraordinary difficulty. As they both felt a short married happiness, they made the most of their moments together and did not selfishly indulge the small annoyances and tiffs common in marriage.

After the ceremony, Isabel and John settled in at Priesthill. While taking stock of the house and arranging her belongings, Janet peeked through the door. Isabel beckoned her to come in, but Janet approached very shyly, almost afraid, with her hands over her face. She left just enough room to peek out to see where she was going. At just four years old, the prospect of a new mother must have been frightening and a little overwhelming.

---

4. A. Sinclair Horne, *Torchbearers of the Truth: Sketches of the Scottish Covenanters* (Edinburgh: Scottish Reformation Society, 1968).

A. B. Todd vividly recounts the scene.[5]

Going up to Isabel, Janet bashfully said, "They say ye are my mither."

To this Isabel responded lovingly with understanding of the confusion and difficulty of the situation for Janet, "What if I should be your mither?"

"Naething, but if I thocht ye were my mither, I would like to come in aside you a wee." Janet clearly longed for a mother's love.

"I hope I will be your mither, sweet bairn, and that God will give me grace to be so, and that you will be a comfort to me and your father," Isabel answered with love and in the faith that God covered this family with His grace and strength.

Thus, Janet and Isabel became mother and daughter indeed. They grew to love each other and enjoy each other's company on the long nights when John was away. Janet now had a mother to teach and train her in the womanly arts. Isabel had a little friend to shepherd in their lonely spot in the moors.

When John would travel, Janet watched and waited for his return. Upon his appearance, she would announce the happy news, run to help him unload his horse, and bring in his load. Isabel prepared warm water for John to wash, re-build the fire, and set out a bowl of fresh porridge ready to greet

---

5. A. B. Todd, *The Homes, Haunts, and Battlefields of the Covenanters* (Edinburgh: Gemmell, 1886), 9–10.

him when he entered the door.[6] This must have been a truly happy time in John Brown's life.

---

6. According to Dane Love, John Brown's porridge bowl still survives, preserved in the Baird Institute Museum in Cumnock. It is made of wood and is cracked. Some claim that the crack was caused by the bullet that shot him, but it is more likely to have cracked when the timber dried out.

SIX

THE CAMERONIANS

IN 1679 WITH THE killing of Archbishop Sharp, conditions for the Covenanters worsened considerably. Sharp originally stood with the Covenanter party. But whatever his motives, he finally chose the politically safe pathway, accepting a government approved prelacy. Biblically Reformed-minded people all over Europe for some time had questioned the church forms prescribed by Roman Catholicism. Questioning Rome ordinarily brought violent reaction, including executions, assassinations or open warfare. Though the English church separated from Rome, it retained much of Rome's *ecclesiology*—doctrines and organizational structures of the church. English Episcopacy maintained Rome's heavy top-down authority and enforcement of its authority by violence. In turn, to abandon the Biblical faith of the Covenanters—including their view of church and civil government—as Archbishop Sharp did, meant treason and an act of war to them. On this ground, a band of Covenanters attacked his coach on May 3, 1679. They dragged him out of the coach and killed him. In reaction, the Scottish government increased their military force against the Covenanters by raising a standing army, effectively establishing marshal law, which the Covenanters would take as a further tyranny.

Seizing the opportunity to share their dismay at the Scottish government's policies, a group of Covenanter pastors and leaders composed a manifesto of allegiance to the Covenant and denounced the policies of Charles II. They met at Rutherglen at a conventicle on May 29, 1679, and, as token of their fervor and strength of conviction, burned these oppressive legal acts of the Scottish government in protest. Drawing upon the popular enthusiasm for the Covenanter movement, a conventicle of about 1,000 people met on June 1 in Drumclog, several miles north of Priesthill. Unfortunately, they suddenly encountered uninvited guests. John Graham of Claverhouse, attacked the gathering but soon found his soldiers bogged down at the edge of a marsh and vulnerable. The Covenanters killed thirty-six soldiers and wounded many more. Claverhouse barely escaped with his life. Imagine sending an army to attack a gathering of Christians worshippers. This is how far the controversy had come. How often in history have matters of conscience led to authoritarian push-back and violence?

The Covenanters' success and further hope of throwing off the tyranny swelled their rebel army to about 6,000 men. The Scottish government then raised an army of more than 10,000 soldiers led by the Duke of Monmouth to subdue the Covenanters. The two armies met at Bothwell Bridge on June 22 and ended with the defeat of the Covenanters and the capture of 1,200 men. The government executed seven but released 500 upon their promising to abandon the rebellion. They deported 200 of the prisoners to the English colony at Barbados in the American Caribbean. In one of the most tragic incidences of the Covenanter movement, the ship carrying the men wrecked and everyone drowned. Due to the poor record-keeping and communication at the time, years passed before some of the wives and families learned the fate of their loved ones. Some families never knew of the shipwreck but waited for years in hopes that their loved ones might return.

Due to John Brown's fervent passion and involvement in the Covenanter movement, many mistakenly believe that he took part in these battles. However, by this time, John was 52 years old and a peaceable man. He may even have held a conscientious objection to these battles. The historic Reformed and Covenanter Biblical view allows defensive wars. However, all Biblical Christians may not agree as to *when* undertaking warfare is wise. All records indicate that John had no desire for violence, but only the freedom to worship as he chose.

A man named John Brown *was* present at the Battle of Drumclog. This is no surprise since John Brown was then a very common name. Many believe the man present at the battle was actually John Brown of Blackwood, one often confused with John Brown of Priesthill since they both lived in the same general area. John Brown of Blackwood was also a passionate Covenanter, but known to be more active in the rebellion.

The Declaration of Rutherglen and the Battle of Bothwell Bridge together marked a critical juncture in the Covenanter struggle, with both sides escalating their efforts. Following the defeat at Bothwell Bridge, two Covenanters, Richard Cameron, a charismatic leader, and Donald Cargill, rose as leaders in the struggle. A small group of Cameron's followers took the name Cameronians.

During the Drumclog and Bothwell Bridge conflicts, Cameron had quietly studied for his ordination in Rotterdam, Holland. Upon his return home, the well-educated minister with degrees from the Scottish St. Andrews University won many followers with his fiery preaching style and strength of conviction. His sermons "burned like flame and smote like a hammer".[1] With the insight of a close friend, John Brown said on occasion that he believed Cameron the "very voice of God for his generation."[2]

The Cameronians declared their intent to make Scotland a "godly" estate and fought to gain control of the country by publicly denouncing the government's initiatives against Presbyterianism.[3] On June 22, 1680, Cameron, Cargill, and their band of followers, numbering around twenty-one men armed with swords, rode to the small town of Sanquhar where a revered cross stood. The men sang a psalm and read a Declaration disowning Charles II as King and proclaiming their intent to fight for the Covenanter cause. They then posted this paper, known as the Sanquhar Declaration, to the cross and rode away, fully prepared to do battle against all

---

1. Harry William Lowe, *Scottish Heroes: Tales of the Covenanters*. (Mountain View, CA: Pacific Press, 1950), 108.

2. Jock Purves, *Sweet Believing: Eight Character Studies of the Scottish Covenanters* (Stirling, Scotland: Stirling Tract Enterprise, 1948), 44.

3. James McCartney, *Ages of Darkness and Blood: A Guide to the Muirkirk Martyrs* (self-published pamphlet, no date), 5.

who disputed their position. The Declaration reads in part:

> Although we be for government and governors such as
> the Word of God and our Covenant allows, yet we for
> ourselves and all that will adhere to us, as the repre-
> sentative of the true Presbyterian Kirk and Covenanted
> nation of Scotland, considering the great hazard of
> lying under such a sin any longer, do by this present dis-
> own Charles Stuart, that has been reigning—or rather
> tyrannising, as we may say—on the throne of Britain
> these years bygone, as having any right, title to, or inter-
> est in the Crown of Scotland. We declare that several
> years since he should have been denuded of being King,
> ruler, or magistrate, or of having any power to act or
> to be obeyed as such. As also we being under the stan-
> dard of our Lord Jesus Christ, Captain of Salvation, do
> declare war with such a tyrant and usurper and all the
> men of his practice, as enemies to our Lord Jesus Christ
> and His cause and Covenants, and against such as have
> strengthened him, sided with or anywise acknowledged
> him in his tyranny civil or ecclesiastic.[4]

The king's Scottish troops killed Richard Cameron in a
bloody skirmish at Airds Moss, near Muirkirk in July of 1680.
To this day, history remembers Cameron as the "Lion of the
Covenant," a man who endowed the movement with clear

---

4. Hector Macpherson, *The Scottish Church Crisis* (London: Hodder
and Stoughton, 1904).

ideals and aims. Upon his death, the responsibility of leading the Covenanter struggle fell to Donald Cargill. In October of 1680, Cargill excommunicated King Charles and other state officials who did not support the Covenanter cause. While some believed this to be a foolish action on his part, Cargill and his followers believed the judgment necessary to reestablishing the Presbyterian Church in Scotland.

In 1681, the soldiers captured Cargill at Covington Mill in Lanarkshire and executed him in Edinburgh. Cargill, an older man, preached the Word of God for over thirty years with the threat of capture and death over him. Before he died, he told his friends that he would soon go to be with the Lord and that he was ready. Cargill penned his own declaration, the Queensferry Paper. Here is an excerpt:

> We reject the king and those associate with him in government from being our king and rulers, being no more bound to them. They have altered and destroyed the Lord's established religion—overturned the fundamental and established laws of the kingdom—taken away altogether Christ's church government, and changed the civil government of this land, which was by a king and free parliament into tyranny. . . . We bind and oblige ourselves to defend ourselves and one another in our worshipping of God, in our natural, civil and divine rights and liberties, till we shall overcome, or send them down under debate to posterity—that they may begin where we end.[5]

---

5. Macpherson, *The Scottish Church Crisis*.

In 1681, the leadership in Scotland changed. The Duke of Monmouth had held the office, under King Charles II, of Lord High Commissioner for years, but as a Protestant, he had not enforced the laws against Covenanters as strongly as King Charles wished, and so he banished the duke. Charles appointed James, Duke of York, to replace Monmouth. James remained loyal to the Catholic Church and came into office with the primary aim of returning Scotland to its Catholic roots. As one of his first acts in office, he instituted a new measure against the Covenanters—the Test Act:

> I...swear I...sincerely profess the true Protestant Religion contained in the Confession of Faith recorded in the first Parliament of King James the Sixth [1567]... shall adhere thereto...educate my children therein... never consent to any change thereto; renounce all such principles inconsistent with the said...Religion and Confession...; affirm...the King's Majesty is the only supream Governour...in all causes ecclesiastical as weill as civil...; renounce...all foreign jurisdictions...; judge it unlawful...to enter into covenants...or to... assemble...in assemblies...to treat...in any matter of State...without his Majestie's special command... or to take up arms against the King...; that there lyes no obligation on me from the National Covenant or the Solemn League and Covenant or any other...to endeavour any change or alteration in the Government either in Church or State...; shall mantein...and...

never decline his Majestie's Power and Jurisdiction...;
swear that this is my oath...without any equivoca-
tion, mental reservation or any manner of evasion
whatsoever.[6]

Established in 1681, this Act meant that all holders of public
offices in church and state must proclaim loyalty to Charles
as head of the church and oppose all attempts to change the
church structure upon pain of death. This marked the beginning of an increased interval of violence in Scottish history
now known as the Killing Times.

6. J. King Hewison, *The Covenanters: A History of the Church of
Scotland from the Reformation to the Revolution, in Two Volumes*, Vol. 2
(Glasgow: John Smith and Son, 1913), 352.

SEVEN

The Boy Preacher

AFTER THE EXECUTIONS OF Cameron and Cargill, but before John and Isabel's wedding, many Covenanters decided to form a group known as the United Societies. This organization met regularly to hear sermons and the latest news in their struggle.

The first *general meeting* took place about ten miles northeast of Muirkirk at Logan farm in Lesmahagow on December 15, 1681. All attendees subscribed to the conviction that King Charles II no longer deserved their allegiance. The group posted a *Declaration* describing the "Aims of the Societies" at Lanark on January 12, 1682. By 1683, Covenanters had established eighty different units with a total of over 7,000 members.

On March 15, 1682, just one month before John and Isabel's wedding, the United Societies held their second meeting, a convention for delegates from all units. They met to discuss official Society business. John Brown hosted this convention at his home in Priesthill. More than likely, they chose Priesthill due to its relative security in its seclusion and John's hospitality.

Following this convention, the Societies met again on October 12, 1682, and resolved to send a few young men to seminary in Holland, to schools sympathetic to their cause.

The members of the Societies, including John, were by no means wealthy men, yet collectively they contributed sacrificially for the education of an ordained minister. By this time, they had lost all the ministers, either by government execution or through accepting governmental pardons (indulgences). And so they found themselves in great need of spiritual leadership. Among several other young men, the Societies selected James Renwick to attend the University of Groningen in the Netherlands. He would soon rise as a primary leader to the Covenanters.

Renwick came into this life on February 15, 1662, amid the Covenanter struggle. He grew up the son of humble parents with strong faith. Prior to his birth, Renwick's mother Elizabeth gave birth to several children who died in infancy. She prayed that God would give her a child who would live to serve God, and He answered her prayers. His father, a weaver, died when Renwick was fourteen but lived long enough to recognize his son's special aptitude for spiritual leadership.

Contributions of friends enabled James Renwick to study at the University of Edinburgh. Though qualifying for his undergraduate degree, Renwick refused to accept it. The government conditioned the degree upon an oath of allegiance to King Charles's government. In good conscience, he could not do this, though he did finally receive his degree privately a few years later. Renwick did not at first embrace the Covenanter cause, but only until after he began his detailed theological studies of the Bible. In meeting in secret with Covenanter ministers, he became convicted of the supremacy of

God over the authority of any established state church. At 19 years old, he witnessed the execution of Cargill and decided to enter the ministry. He said later that Cargill's last words made a powerful impact upon him:

> As to the causes of my suffering, the chief is—not acknowledging the present Authority, as it is established in the Supremacy and Explanatory Act. This is the magistracy I have resisted, that which is invested with Christ's power. Seeing that power taken from Christ, which is His glory, and made the essential of an earthly crown, it seemed to me as if one were wearing my husband's garments, after he had killed him. There is no distinction we can make, that can free the acknowledger from being a partaker of this sacrilegious robbing of God. And it is but to cheat our consciences to acknowledge the civil power alone, that it is of the essence of the crown; and seeing they are so express, we ought to be plain; for otherwise, we deny our testimony and consent that Christ be robbed of His glory.[1]

Aware that the Societies needed an ordained minister to lead them, Renwick whole-heartedly pursued his studies, finishing the required courses within a year's time. The depth of study required to receive ordination was then, as now,

---

1. Thomas Houston, *The Life of James Renwick: A Historical Sketch of His Life, Labours and Martyrdom and a Vindication of His Character and Testimony* (n.p.: James A. Dickson Books, 1983), 10.

very intense. This fact makes his accomplishment the more remarkable and commendable. While in Holland, Renwick wrote this passage describing his longing to return to the Societies:

> My longings and earnest desire to be in that land, and with the pleasant remnant, are very great. I cannot tell what may be in it, but I hope the Lord hath either some work to work, or else is minded presently to call for a testimony at my hand. If He give me frame and furniture, I desire to welcome either of them.[2]

As Renwick studied faithfully in Holland, he found a mentor in Robert Hamilton, with whom Renwick continued to correspond throughout his ministry. Hamilton's sponsorship readily enabled Renwick's ordination in Holland. Thus, he quickly returned to Scotland and the United Societies. Arriving in the Fall of 1683, Renwick began his Scottish ministry.

The Society continued to meet and support one another during Renwick's absence. In January of 1683, they collected an offering to help support families in need. Also in 1683, the society sent a letter to their fellow believers in Ireland and composed a document of questions and answers that would define them as an organization.

Even during this time when the Covenanters suffered under such great scrutiny, the Brown family, ever true to the Scottish ways, held hospitality dear as a necessary vir-

---

2. Houston, *The Life of James Renwick.*

tue and standard for the household. The Browns welcomed all travelers with food, drink, and a place to rest if needed. The family conducted themselves with proper defensive concern and prudence around the visiting strangers. But they also conducted themselves with grace, deeply mindful of the pressing need of so many people in those days. A great many of these travelers were fellow Covenanters. The little cottage welcomed and served its visitors as well as it could with a fire on its clay floor and with its humble provisions.

One stormy night during the fall (of 1683, possibly), Isabel and Janet stayed at home with the newest member of the family—a baby boy named John. The mother and child combed wool recently shorn from their flocks in preparation for weaving cloth to sell at the market. Isabel nursed baby by the fire with the dog lying at her feet. Suddenly, the dog sprang up with fervor and ran barking towards the door. Thinking her father approached, Janet called off the dog and ran out to greet him. Instead, she returned to the cottage shyly leading a strange man.

Isabel felt a twinge of worry. She could not know whether this stranger might be an informant for the crown. She knew John would soon be home, and that he could be in jeopardy. The man appeared very young with an attractive air about him, but his clothes spoke of fatigue and difficult travels. Adding to her suspicions that he might be a spy, Isabel noticed a discrepancy between how his educated speech sounded and the humble clothes he wore.

Blissfully unaware of her mother's worries, five-year-old

Janet welcomed the man with warm hospitality as she had learned by example. She offered him John's chair by the fire, the best seat in the house. With this, Isabel noticed the man seemed genuinely affected. She relaxed a little with this observation and sang a lullaby to her baby as he fell asleep. The man's spirits visibly lifted while she sang. He clearly accepted Janet's eager help with grace. She helped him out of his wet shawl and treated him just as she had often seen Isabel treat John after coming in from a tough night. Watching her made Isabel smile as she realized how much Janet gleaned from watching her parents together.

Observing how kindly and gently Janet treated him, he started to tear up as he said: "May the blessings of him that is ready to perish rest upon you, my dear bairn. Surely God has heard my cry, and provided me a place to rest my head for a night. O that I had in the wilderness a lodging-place of wayfaring men, that I might leave my people and go from them; for there be an assembly of treacherous men."[3]

The door swung open at this moment as John walked in, startled at the sight of a man by the fire. He looked the man in the face and suddenly softened. To this, the man said, "Do you know me?"

"I think I do," John said. "It was in this house that the Societies met that contributed to send you to Holland, and now I fear they have not received you (at least some of them) as they ought."

---

3. McGavin, *Memoirs of John Brown*, 20.

Thus, James Renwick stayed and rested with the Browns for a few nights while his strength returned. He and John enjoyed Christian fellowship and conversation about Renwick's experiences in Holland and while traveling, and John updated Renwick on the state of Covenanters locally. Though perhaps upon an uneven start, Renwick eventually assumed leadership of the United Societies and remained a steadfast Covenanter minister throughout.

Those who knew Renwick during this time described him as a "catholic, genial, loving spirit."[4] He was "catholic" in the broad sense of belonging to the universal church of Christian believers. Many of his letters survive to this day, and in reading them, one can clearly see he was a faithful friend with an ardent desire to restore the church. As he penned,

> We are not a Church at present, and cannot act fully as an organized Church. We are a broken, persecuted remnant. Our societies are not a Church, but a temporary means of enjoying proper religious instruction and ordinances of worship. They are, besides, associations for self-defence, and for watching and taking advantage of any public movement for overturning the present despotism, and recovering our liberties, civil and religious. We require to make the terms of admission strict, to guard against spies, and those who are contentious or quarrelsome. At the same time they declare the close and hallowed relations that bound them to all the true disci-

4. Houston, *The Life of James Renwick*, 55.

ples of their common Lord. In a noble spirit of Christian brotherhood, they virtually proclaim, "On the communion of saints, let us impose no new restrictions. Though others differ from us in the word of their special testimony, let us embrace and love them, and acknowledge fellowship with them as Christian brethren."[5]

---

5. Houston, *The Life of James Renwick*, 66–67.

EIGHT

CHRISTIAN FELLOWSHIP

THE ADVENT OF THE 1680s marked a dangerous period in John's life. Laws against Covenanters grew stronger, and it became more difficult for John to pursue his vocation. Patrols roamed the area ready to question suspicious people on any whim.

John Brown made the fateful decision to withdraw from the State Church of Scotland. On September 19, 1680, the curate wrote in the church roll:

> Present the minister and all the elders except Grinok Mains . . . It was delated that Johne broune in Priesthilles, Thomas Richart in Mains, and Jane Weir in Darnhunch would not attend the public ordinances.[1]

Again on November 11 of the same year, the curate confirmed John Brown's decision:

> Thus we went to Johne broune, I myself being present; gave his ressones first that I kepit cumpani with the indulgit ministers; next that I paid Sesse [cess],[2]

---

1. J. King Hewison, "The Martyrdom of John Brown" in *United Free Church Magazine,* 1906, 19.

2. *Cess* was a tax for pay of crown-soldiers, and war. The Covenanters claimed the cess levied money to the purpose of destroying Presbyterian-

which it being denyit from hus as not being sufficient
groundes to make separatione, the resones which he
gave was that he whom he lookit as the treu messenger
of Jesus Christ, who is now laying at Arsmoss (Richard
Cameron), denounced and dischargit all as they would
answer in the great day, he never should heir any of
thes indulgit persones; therefore he would not: as far as
Thomas Richart, he is cum in again to the [Church].[3]

For the sake of survival, John then ceased to work as a
Carrier. Upon leaving the state church, he became a *criminal*.
If knowledge or suspicions existed regarding a band of soldiers in the area, John would hide in the moors and caves of
Ayrshire. Being hilly country, there were several ravines and
caves where he could go unnoticed while troops scoured the
countryside for "rebels."

After John left his life's work, the little family supported
themselves with their farm and more than likely worked
together with other Covenanter families to ensure that they
mutually met both their own and each other's needs. The
Covenanter wives and children must have found strength in
mutual company as they walked this lonely road together.

James Renwick continued to make waves as the leader of
the United Societies and, by default, the Covenanter movement. He led the Societies in penning the Apologetical Declaration in 1684. This Declaration made it known that they

---

ism, the Covenant, and therefore the Gospel itself.

3. Hewison, "The Martyrdom of John Brown," 19.

would not hesitate to kill anyone who traitorously informed against them or hunted them. This may have made informers fear the Covenanters, but more so served to anger the soldiers.

The Scottish government retaliated against the Declaration by instituting the infamous Oath of Abjuration on November 22, 1684. The Oath required questioning all suspected persons and forcing them to renounce the Apologetical Declaration. Suspects must pledge never to raise arms against the king. The authorities would answer any refusal to take the Oath with immediate execution—the suspect, his wife, and his children. The Oath declared:

> I... do hereby abhor, renounce, and disown, in the presence Almighty God, the pretended declaration of war lately affixed at several parish churches, in so far as it declares a war against his sacred Majesty, and asserts that it is lawful to kill such as serve his Majesty in church, state, army, or country, or such as act against the authors of the pretended declaration... I... disown the villainous authors thereof.[4]

John Brown's welfare and life suffered even greater threat in 1684 when his name appeared on the list of fugitives in the Royal Proclamation of May 5. John's name appeared because he did not attend the established church but rather gave aid to Covenanter ministers. He took to the hills ever more often, becoming extremely wary and cautious in his

---

4. Hewison, *The Covenanters*, 442.

travels. He could not afford to draw any attention to himself. Since the troops often recruited local spies to help find these fugitives, all the Covenanters must exert extreme caution in their movements.

One day on hearing of the presence of troops, John fled to a ravine for safety. He made his way to a hiding place and began to pray. As he started praying, he heard voices singing nearby. John made his way over to where the voices were and found his dear friends, William and David Steel. The Steels, close neighbors to the Browns, taught Sunday School with John. Overjoyed at the sight of his friends, John eagerly joined in the singing.

David Steel, a man of average height with blue eyes and blonde hair, lived in Lesmahagow, while William Steel lived in Waterhead. History is not clear regarding the relation of the two Steel men. Some accounts list them as brothers while others describe them as cousins. Regardless, they had a close relationship with each other and with John Brown. Both Steels fought at the Covenanter movement's critical Battle of Bothwell Bridge and continued with deep commitment to the Covenanter cause. History remembers David, especially, for his dedication and godliness. Due to their involvement in the Covenanter uprisings, the Steels spent most of their time on the run. Many believe that David's wife, Mary Weir and Isabel Brown may have been relatives. At the least, Isabel counted Mary Steel as a close friend.

David related to John that the king's forces nearly captured him the day before. The soldiers quietly approached as he led family worship. Fortunately, someone noticed the soldiers drawing near and alerted the household. With no time to run or find good hiding, David put his Bible on his chest and lay in the cow's feed. His wife quickly covered him with hay. The soldiers came in and searched the house thoroughly, even stabbing into the hay to make sure David did not hide in it. Fortunately, the sword struck his Bible and he remained uninjured. After the close encounter, David and William decided it would be safer for their families and themselves if they went into hiding for a while.

John and the Steels spent the rest of the day in worship and prayer as they read their Bibles and sang psalms aloud. This time of worship and fellowship strengthened and encouraged them as they continued together through the night. When morning came, William crept out of the ravine to scout for any soldiers remaining nearby. Discovering the soldiers had departed, the three Covenanters left their hiding place to the unexpected sound of a sweet voice singing,

> O let the prisoners' sighs ascend
> Before Thy sight on high;
> Preserve those by Thy mighty power
> That are design'd to die.

Looking about they could find no one at all. They took the singing as a special sign of God's favor in this time of trial. Reacting to this extraordinary occurrence, John Brown said to the Steels,

Whoever or wherever, the words come from, we have little concern, one thing we may take comfort from, they are God's words to His Church in affliction; and that is our situation. Who lye among the pots? We scullions, black in the opinion of our enemies. But God sees us not as man sees us, but compares us to doves; doves on the wing, whose feathers of gold and silver are best seen while they fly. It may be, we are on the wing to an eternal world, and this Bethel meeting is preparing us to mount up with wings like eagles. If so, let us keep in mind, that we have nothing to boast of, but grace, grace; unto it is our acknowledgement.[5]

Years later, William Steel said if there was a night in his life he would like to live over again, it would be that one.

Many Covenanters would now lose their lives under the Oath of Abjuration's mandatory and summary penalty. In August of 1684, the two brothers John and William Campbell walked home to Wellwood. Troopers stopped them as they approached their home and questioned their beliefs. Upon discovering the brothers' Covenanter roots, the soldiers tortured them without mercy. William soon after died of his injuries, but John lived to avenge his brother's senseless death. Later after the Glorious Revolution placed William and Mary on the throne and restored Presbyterianism to Scotland, John Campbell would lead a Scottish regiment.

---

5. Edward Miller, *Martyrs of the Moors; Scottish Covenant Heroes* (London: Pilgrim Press, 1908), 93–94.

His troop flew a banner proclaiming "Moorkirk, God and Country" with 1689 imprinted, highlighting the time of the Glorious Revolution.[6]

Every Covenanter family felt their beliefs strongly and expressed them as best they could. In 1685, a group of fifteen teenage girls in Pentland met to pray for the cause. In creating their group, they wrote this covenant,

> This is a Covenant made between the Lord and us, with our whole hearts, and to give up ourselves feely to Him without reserve, soul and body, hearts and affections, to be His children and Him to be our God and Father; if it please the Lord to send His gospel to the land again, that we stand to this Covenant which we have written, between the Lord and us, as we shall answer at that great day. That we shall never break this Covenant which we have made between the Lord and us, that we shall stand to this Covenant which we have made; and if not, it shall be a witness against us in the great day when we shall stand before the Lord and His holy angels. O Lord, give us real grace in our hearts this day to mend Zion's breaches which are in such low case this day; and make us to mourn with her, for Thou hast said them that mourn with her in the time of trouble shall rejoice when she rejoiceth, when the Lord shall bring

---

6. John Macintosh, *Ayrshire Nights' Entertainments: A Descriptive Guide to the History, traditions, Antiquities &c., of the County of Ayr* (Kilmarnock, Scotland: Dunlop & Drennan, 1894), 239.

back the captivity of Zion, when He shall deliver her out of her enemies' hand, when her King shall come and raise her from the dust, in spite of all her enemies that oppose her, either devils or men. That thus they have banished their King, Christ, out of the land, yet He will arise and avenge His children's blood at their enemies' hands, which cruel murderers have shed.[7]

---

7. Jerri Faris, *Covenanters of Scotland: A History for Children* (Pittsburgh, PA: Crown & Covenant Publications, 1995), 7–8.

NINE

Bloody Clavers

ONE OF THE MOST notorious persecutors of the Covenanters was John Graham of Claverhouse. Claverhouse, born in 1648 in Glen Ogilvy in the northerly lowlands, possessed respectable roots, wealth, and family connections. The family boasted of a relation to the Duke of Montrose.

A few surviving paintings furnish historians a fair portrait of Claverhouse's appearance. Parts of his armor also exist to this day, backing up several claims that he was a very small man. John Morrison, speaking to Sir Walter Scott, said this of Claverhouse's appearance:

> He [Claverhouse] attending the murder of two martyrs on the sands of Dumfries, rode his horse along the coping of a parapet wall built to guard off the waters of the Nith in time of floods, and when the horse had arrived at one end, he wheeled round on one of his hind legs as on a pivot, repeating the same manoeuvre. His arms were long, and reached to his knees, his hair red or frizzly, and his look altogether diabolical. Such would never be the face that painters love to limn and ladies to look on.[1]

---

1. Hewison, *The Covenanters*, 297.

Claverhouse attended the University of St. Andrews in Scotland and then served in the French and Dutch armies. While serving in the Dutch army, he acted as a bodyguard for the young Prince William of Orange, even saving his life during a battle in 1674. After his distinguished service in Holland, Claverhouse received several respectable offers to establish his career as a soldier there. However, he denied these offers in favor of returning to his homeland.

In 1677, he returned to Scotland with a dashing reputation. The Privy Council had heard tales of his bravery and were eager to add him to their ranks. On September 23, 1678, he received commission to lead a troop of Highlanders infamous for brashness and ill-manners. In the same year, as commander of the Independent Troop of Horse and under orders from the Scottish Privy Council, Claverhouse led the Highlander invasion of Covenanter homes—a dubious task for a Christian soldier. Further illustrating his character, Claverhouse ordered Gilbert McMichen of New Glenluce to board his troops free of charge.[2] When the Highlanders finally returned to the north, Claverhouse and his men had relieved McMichen's home of all the possessions and food they could carry. One account says they left with "three horses, worth ten pounds each."[3]

---

2. According to Dane Love, this is only one of thousands of similar examples—the "Highland Host" were quartered across Ayrshire too, and may even have been quartered in John Brown's house.

3. McGavin, *Memoirs of John Brown*, 30–31.

On December 28, 1678, Claverhouse wrote this passage to his commanding officer, the Earl of Linlithgow:

My Lord, I came here [the Black Bull Inn in Moffat] last night with the troop and am just going to march for Dumfries, where I resolve to quarter the whole troop. . . . I am informed since I came that this county has been very loose. On Tuesday was eight days, and Sunday, there were great field conventicles just by here, with great contempt of the regular clergy; who complain extremely that I have no orders to aprehend anybody for past demeanours. And besides that, all the particular orders I have being contained in that order of quartering, every place where we quarter we must see them, which makes them fear the less. I am informed that the most convenient posts for quartering the dragoons will be Moffat, Lochmaben and Annan; whereby the whole county will be kept in awe. Besides that, my lord, they tell me that the end of the bridge of Dumfries is in Galloway, and that they may hold conventicles at our nose, we dare not dissipate them, seeing our orders confine us to Dumfries and Annandale. Such an insult as that would not please me; and, on the other hand, I am unwilling to exceed orders, so that I expect from your lordship orders how to carry in such cases.[4]

---

4. Dane Love, *Scottish Covenanter Stories: Tales from the Killing Times.* (Glasgow: Neil Wilson Pub., 2000), 39–40.

Soon after this letter, Claverhouse received permission to add Galloway to his territory of exposing and punishing Covenanters. In Lesmahagow, he established a garrison to make it easier for him to make his raids in the area. After his defeat at Drumclog in 1679, Claverhouse resolved to vindicate himself by chasing down Covenanters relentlessly. On January 31, 1682, his superiors extended his powers to persecute them. He received these orders to pursue and punish:

> Several persons of disaffected and seditious principles in the shires of Wigtown and Dumfries, and the Stewartries of Kirkcudbright and Annandale, who have for disquiet and disturbance of the peace for divers years past deserted the public ordinances in their parish churches, haunted and frequented rebellious field conventicles, and committed divers other disorders of that nature.[5]

The Privy Council deemed the Sheriff of Galloway too lenient toward the Covenanters. They desired instead a tougher enforcer of their policies against the consciences of the people. Claverhouse received promotion as the Sheriff of Galloway in 1682. After this expansion of his power, Claverhouse suspended the pay of his soldiers, instead telling them to provide for themselves by what they could steal from the Covenanter families.[6] He would often listen to the roll call at

---

5. Love, *Scottish Covenanter Stories*, 40–41.

6. The Bible countenances taking of spoil from vanquished invaders in a defensive war (e.g., Judges 11:12–32). Plundering one's fellow citizens

church and then set out to apprehend the absent parishioners. The churches filled with terrified citizens, but the staunchest Covenanters slipped into hiding. Claverhouse often bribed citizens to spy for him.

He also made frequent use of brutal tactics to find the hiding Covenanters. For example, he would round up young children and line them in front of a firing squad. He then would order the soldiers to shoot above their heads while he yelled and asked them to divulge their parents' whereabouts. Not surprisingly, preying on the fear of young children worked. Of course, this heartless tactic left the children feeling guilty for the rest of their lives by the subsequent capture of their parents. The Ettrick Shepherd described Claverhouse as possessing "the nature of a wolf, if he had the bravery of a bulldog."[7]

In March of 1682, Claverhouse wrote this passage describing a chase of Covenanters:

> I am just beginning to send out many parties, finding the rebels become secure, and the country so quiet in all appearance. I sent out a party with my brother Dave three nights ago. The first night he took Drumbui and one Maclellan, and the great villain MacClorg, the smith at Minnigaff that made all the clikys, and after whom the forces have trotted so often. It cost me

on the grounds of the conviction of conscience might be described as nothing less than barbarous.

7. Todd, *The Homes, Haunts, and Battlefields of the Covenanters*, 13.

both pains and money to know how to find him: I am resolved to hang him; for it is necessary I make some example of severity, lest rebellion be thought cheap here. There cannot be alive a more wicked fellow. [MacClorg ended up escaping yet again.][8]

In December of 1682, Claverhouse went up against Sir John Dalrymple, a man of wealthy family and high standing within the country. Dalrymple felt Claverhouse overly cruel toward the Covenanters in his town. Dalrymple himself had already meted out punishment to the Covenanters, but then Claverhouse felt it was not enough and added his own punishments. When Dalrymple disagreed, Claverhouse wrote a letter to the Privy Council denouncing him as a sympathizer. Believing Claverhouse their field commander and strongest enforcer, the Council quickly entertained his claims. In response to the immense fines the Privy Council imposed on him, Dalrymple refused to pay, but rather sought refuge in Holland. If the well-regarded aristocrat Sir John Dalrymple could not stand before him, no one was safe in Claverhouse's Scotland.

While patrolling in 1682,[9] Claverhouse came upon William Graham in Galloway. Graham left his mother's house to hide from the patrols he knew were in the area. Espying Graham, Claverhouse pursued him across the moors. With Claverhouse's overcoming him, Graham attempted to sur-

---

8. Love, *Scottish Covenanter Stories*, 41.

9. Or possibly 1684.

render. With no regard to his words and without warning, Claverhouse summarily and fatally shot him.[10]

On April 13, 1683, the Privy Council passed a law forbidding even *speaking* with a Covenanter. With this law, they offered their last "act of mercy," allowing Covenanters to come forward to take the 1681 test of loyalty, and, in passing its requirements, receive indemnity. This offer would expire on August 1.

As a reward for his success in curbing the Covenanter Movement, in May of 1683, Claverhouse received a seat on the Scottish Privy Council. He now possessed great power within and over Scotland. As part of the Privy Council, he would now contribute to the passage of increasingly harsh laws and horrific punishments to pour out on the Covenanters. The Council strengthened church attendance laws. In concert, the Anglican clergy warned against falsification of records. To ensure the clergy followed the Privy Council's demands, they mandated all church officers themselves to take the Test and to renew previous certification, that they explicitly declare their aversion to Presbyterianism.

Claverhouse and other members of the Privy Council began in June 1683 to comb through church attendance rolls.

---

10. Hewison, *The Covenanters*, 376. The records from different prominent historians show confusion as to what year this actually took place. A primary reason for this confusion is that William Graham had a brother named James who was executed under Claverhouse's orders following a trial in Edinburgh. Their close relation, same last names, and similar circumstances have resulted in confusion within the historical record.

They summoned the absent members to take the Test. Those who refused, publicly doubted, or successfully hid from the authorities found themselves listed in the National Fugitive Roll. In total, 180 names appeared upon this list of church non-attenders declared criminals and eligible of execution on sight. One name on this list was John Brown of Priesthill.

In September of 1683, Claverhouse and the Privy Council extended the Test deadline for another six months. However, following the same meeting, Claverhouse dispensed orders to all officers "to punish with all rigour that our law will allow all such as will refuse this our last offer of mercy."[11] The offer of pardon was now no longer a possibility.

Even as his persecution progressed, Claverhouse courted and married the beautiful Jean Cochrane in 1684. She possessed a royal heritage, the granddaughter of the Earl of Cochrane. However, her family had Covenanter ties, leaving her mother to worry about Jean marrying Claverhouse. Upon hearing of his future mother-in-law's hesitation, Claverhouse penned this telling passage to her:

> For my owen pairt I look on myself as a cleanger. I may cur people guilty of that a cleanser, plaigue of presbytry be conversing with them, but can not be infected, and see very little of that amongst those persons but may be easily rubed of. And for the young ladie herself, I shall answer for her. Had she been right principled she would never in dispyt of her mother and relations made choyse

---

11. Hewison, *The Covenanters*, 392.

of a persicutor, as they call me. So who ever thinks to misrepresent me on that head will fynd them selfs mistaken; for both in the King and Churches interest, dryve as fast as they think fit, they will never see me behind.[12]

Clearly Claverhouse felt he had a sacred calling in his cruelty. To highlight this point, consider his heart and mind on his wedding day, June 10, 1684. Claverhouse heard that James Renwick led a conventicle nearby. Rather than focus attention on his joyful day and new bride, Claverhouse insisted upon riding with soldiers to apprehend the Covenanters.

In the summer of 1684, the Privy Council began an increased commitment to the fight against the Covenanters. Upon Claverhouse's suggestion and urging, the Council passed a law demanding jails to send reports on all prisoners held. They intended that "it may be recommended to the justices to proceed and pronounce sentence of death against them immediately, which sentence they are to cause execute within six hours after pronouncing it (within three hours in Glasgow and Dumfries.)"[13] This act would fulfill a dual purpose. Aside from purging the Covenanter enemy, they would also ease their rapidly growing, overcrowded jails. With this declaration, a new and worse, cold-blooded epoch in Scottish history began.

Renwick led the Covenanters in composing and releasing a summary of their beliefs and intent to defend themselves. They

---

12. Ibid., 425–426.
13. Ibid., 435.

called the resulting document the Apologetical Declaration. The United Societies posted the Declaration on November 8, 1684. An excerpt clearly illustrates the Covenanters' intent:

> Wherein we have disowned the authority of Charles Stewart (not authority of God's institution, either among Christians or heathens) and all authority depending from him'; 'jointly and unanimously...we utterly detest and abhor that hellish principle of killing all who differ in judgment or persuasion from us, it having no bottom upon the word of God, or right reason...to pursue the ends of our Covenants...we... declare...that whosoever stretch forth their hands against us (justiciary, military, assenting gentlemen, "viperous and malicious" clergy, intelligencers, delators, raisers of hue and cry), all and every one of such shall be reputed by us enemies to God and the Covenanted Work of Reformation, and punished as such, according to our power and the degree of their offence.... Finally, we do declare, that we abhor, condemn, and discharge any personal attempts, upon any pretext whatsomever, without previous deliberation, common or competent consent, without certain probation...confession...or the notoriousness of the deeds; and inhibiting private judgments.... A people by holy covenants dedicated unto the Lord...for defending and promoting this glorious work of Reformation.[14]

---

14. Hewison, *The Covenanters*, 440–441.

As may be imagined, this Declaration aroused intense displeasure and reaction from the Privy Council. In their attempt to quell the wave of Covenanter strength, the Council met on November 22 to declare a hostile new law against the Covenanters:

> It being put to the vote in Councell: The Council whether or not any persone who ounes or does not disoune the late extirpation, traitorous declaratione upon oath, whether they have arms or not, should be immediately killed before two witnesses: and the persone or persones who are to have instructions from the Councell to that effect: caryed in the affirmative.[15]

Claverhouse lent a hand in composing this law, and it essentially gave him and other enforcers free reign to murder anyone who would not declare the English and Scottish king to be above all. From this point until the Glorious Revolution of 1688 restoring Presbyterianism to Scotland under William and Mary, anyone suspected of Covenanter allegiance must swear the Oath of Abjuration or immediately die.

This Oath created ripples of incredulousness across Scotland and England not because it was a logical swipe against the offending Covenanters, but because it subordinated the church to the king. In taking the Oath, one attributed all authority over the church to the king. The Oath now began to rouse from their former passivity the many peaceable Cov-

---

15. Ibid.

enanters, those who had not previously joined with their militant counterparts. Though they might not fully agree with the Apologetical Declaration, they could never affirm that the king was the head of the church. A whole new group of Scotsmen would now find themselves enemies of the government by no new action on their own part.

At the end of 1684, Claverhouse fell out of favor with the Privy Council and King Charles. A few of his colleagues jealously felt he had gained too much personal favor of James, the Duke of York and next in line to the throne. In response, his formerly favorable colleagues worked to smear Claverhouse as a shifty officer not to be trusted. The Privy Council removed Claverhouse from their ranks and promoted several officers over him to ensure supervision and his containment. This sequence of events so angered Claverhouse that he strived the harder and more devotedly to seek out Covenanters and to make them pay for their rebellion against state authority.

Claverhouse's vindication came when Charles died of natural causes in 1685. James, Duke of York, took the throne on February 10, 1685 as King James II of England and VII of Scotland. This King James advocated Roman Catholicism unabashedly and would make no pretense regarding his loyalties. His first Scottish Parliament met on April 23. During this meeting, all legislation there favored the new king's desires. James decreed anyone known to attend a Conventicle could be murdered with no accountability. He then appointed Claverhouse as Viscount of Dundee, which gave him greater license and more power than ever to track down and punish the Covenanters.

TEN

A Misty Morning

In the Spring of 1685, the Covenanters were a fractured group fearing for their lives. The United Societies dissolved and Scotland's aristocratic lords had killed or imprisoned many key leaders, both pastoral and military leaders.

On April 26, a young man named James Nisbet attended a conventicle led by John Brown's friend Alexander Peden in Ayrshire. As the group worshipped, Claverhouse and his Highlanders suddenly ambushed them. This set off a long, arduous chase that ended on April 30, when Nisbet and his fellow Covenanters finally escaped. As Nisbet later wrote, "Within three or four days Graham of Claverhouse, with 100 horse and 300 Highland men... got sight of seven of us... pursued us all that day for thirty-two miles till midnight. We got no refreshment all that day, except a few mouthfuls of bread and cheese and moss water."[1]

Weary from the chase, Claverhouse called off the search and made his way to Lesmahagow, north-northeast of Muirkirk. Peden, feeling reasonably assured of his safety, decided to make his way to Priesthill to spend the night with John and Isabel before he once more moved on.

Peden and John spent much of the night talking and rejoic-

---

1. Hewison, "The Martyrdom of John Brown," 20.

ing in their faith together. More than likely, John had been in hiding for some time, unable to enjoy Christian fellowship. Now to avoid placing the family in too much danger with his presence, Peden planned to leave before sunlight.

The Brown family woke with Peden. That morning came dark and misty—a common occurrence on the Scottish moors. It would provide invisibility to Peden, a blessing. Yet the darkness also held foreboding. Peden declared, "Poor woman, a fearful morning, a fearful morning, a dark, misty morning."[2]

After seeing Peden off, the Browns sat down for breakfast. Then John led them in daily family worship. At such times, the family would sing Psalm 27, most likely from the 1599 Geneva Bible, a version based on William Tyndale's original English translation from the Greek.

PSALM 27 (1599 GENEVA BIBLE)

1. The Lord is my light and my salvation, whom shall I fear? the Lord is the strength of my life, of whom shall I be afraid?
2. When the wicked, even mine enemies and my foes came upon me to eat up my flesh, they stumbled and fell.
3. Though an host pitched against me, mine heart should not be afraid: though war be raised against me, I will trust in this.

---

2. Hewison, "The Martyrdom of John Brown," 21.

4. One thing have I desired of the Lord, that I will require, even that I may dwell in the house of the Lord all the days of my life, to behold the beauty of the Lord, and to visit his Temple.

5. For in the time of trouble He shall hide me in His Tabernacle: in the secret place of His pavilion shall He hide me, and set me up upon a rock.

6. And now shall He lift up mine head above mine enemies round about me: therefore will I offer in His Tabernacle sacrifices of joy: I will sing and praise the Lord.

7. Hearken unto my voice, O Lord, when I cry: have mercy also upon me and hear me.

8. When Thou saidest, Seek ye my face, mine heart answered unto Thee, O Lord, I will seek Thy face.

9. Hide not therefore Thy face from me, nor cast Thy servant away in displeasure: Thou hast been my succor, leave me not, neither forsake me, O God of my salvation.

10. Though my father and my mother should forsake me, yet the Lord will gather me up.

11. Teach me thy way, O Lord, and lead me in a right path, because of mine enemies.

12. Give me not unto the lust of mine adversaries: for there are false witnesses risen up against me, and such as speak cruelly.

13. I should have fainted, except I had believed to see the goodness of the Lord in the land of the living.

14. Hope in the Lord: be strong, and he shall comfort thine heart, and trust in the Lord.

John then led the family in reading John 16 as their daily scriptural passage. More than likely, they read a chapter a day out of the Bible for reflection and study. Here is an excerpt from the 1599 Geneva translation of that passage:

JOHN 16

1. These things have I said unto you, that ye should not be offended.
2. They shall excommunicate you: yea the time shall come, that whosoever killeth you, will think that he doeth God service.
3. And these things will they do unto you, because they have not known the Father, nor Me.
4. But these things have I told you, that when the hour shall come, ye might remember, that I told you them. And these things said I not unto you from the beginning, because I was with you . . .
33. These things have I spoken unto you, that in Me ye might have peace: in the world ye shall have affliction, but be of good comfort: I have overcome the world.

With Peden's departure and finishing their simple breakfast meal of porridge, the family dispersed for their regular activities. John's nephew, John Browning, arrived soon after. He and John went searching on the nearby moors for peat to cut. Scottish families routinely began cutting peat in April and May. The peat—consisting of naturally decomposed plant matter and the sole natural resource on the moor—gave them a free and reliable source of fuel for the winter to come. To prepare peat is involved and lengthy, as it must dry completely. The whole family would have participated in this process.

ELEVEN

No King but Jesus

On that same morning of Alexander Peden's departure from Priesthill—May 1, 1685—a local went to Claverhouse with news of Covenanters in the area. Sensing that these were the same Covenanters he had chased to no avail, Claverhouse eagerly gathered three garrisons of dragoons and set off to apprehend the suspects. Though the morning remained dark and misty, Claverhouse's guide knew the land and understood his neighbors' schedules. Thus, he could take the soldiers through the difficult, boggy terrain, and intelligently estimate the fugitives' whereabouts.

John and his nephew John Browning cut peat out in the moors near the Brown's cottage. John glanced up to the sudden sight of horses and figures moving toward him out of the mist. Alarmed, he knew this must be one of the government's enforcers. The guide came first, closely followed by Claverhouse. That face struck fear to John's heart. The troops surrounded the two men as Claverhouse began to question them.

John immediately formed his resolve as he dropped his spade. Under Claverhouse's orders, he led the troops to his home. By many accounts, he walked "rather like a leader than a captive,"[1] demonstrating his resolute spirit and strength of

---

1. Gilfillan, *The Martyrs, Heroes and Bards*, 88–90.

conviction as he approached the throne of God.

As the men neared the house, Janet saw them and ran inside to warn Isabel. Isabel responded, "The thing that I feared is come upon me; O give me grace for this hour!"[2]

Then she, pregnant with John's second son, rose and grabbed little John's hand to keep him close to her side. The three of them went outside and watched as John approached, leading Claverhouse and his dragoons.

Once at the house, Claverhouse began to question John and his nephew, asking him why he did not attend church. John answered that his Covenanter beliefs made it impossible for him to worship in a church subject to mere human authority. In response to the demand, he refused to take the Abjuration Oath. Claverhouse, dissatisfied with his answers, pressed forward, asking John if he would pray for the king. John said he could recognize no king but Jesus. At this bold statement, Claverhouse asked the guides if John was a Covenanter preacher.

"No, no, he was never a preacher," the guides responded.

Claverhouse responded: "Well, if he has never preached, meikle has he prayed in his time." Then to John, he yelled, "Go to your prayers, for you shall immediately die!"[3]

With this, John fell to his knees and began to pray fervently. His stutter disappeared. He prayed blessings upon his

2. McGavin, *Memoirs of John Brown*, 31–36.

3. J. H. Thomson and Matthew Hutchison. *The Martyr Graves of Scotland* (Edinburgh: Oliphant, Anderson & Ferrier, 1903), 142–146.

wife and children. He especially prayed for Scotland, that God would spare the country and raise up a remnant to stand for Him. As he prayed, some of the dragoons began to shed tears.

Claverhouse, aware of the softening of his dragoons, interrupted John three separate times, saying once, "I gave you leave to pray, and ye've begun to preach."

"Sir, you know neither the nature of preaching nor praying, if you call this preaching," John boldly answered, and then resumed and finished praying.

Claverhouse then quickly commanded, "Take goodnight of your wife and children." [4]

Claverhouse told the young nephew John Browning that if he could offer helpful information, he would spare his life. Terrified, Browning immediately confessed to Claverhouse that he had participated in some raids on the Scottish troops. Claverhouse asked Browning to help search the house for treasonable offenses.

During this exchange, John rose and went to Isabel. He reminded her of what Peden said on their wedding day and said, "Now, Isabel, the day is come that I told you would come, when I spake first to you of marrying me. You see me summoned to appear, in a few minutes, before the court of heaven, as a witness in our Redeemer's cause, against the Ruler of Scotland. Are you willing that I should part from you?"

---

4. Purves, *Sweet Believing*, 38–39.

"Indeed, John, in this cause I am willingly to part with you," Isabel said with tears in her eyes.

"Then that is all my desire," John replied. "I have no more to do but die; for I have been in case to meet death for many years."[5]

He then kissed her, little John, and Janet. He prayed with Isabel, "That every covenanted blessing might be poured upon her and her children, born and unborn, as one refreshed by the influence of the Holy Spirit, when he comes down like rain upon the mown grass, as showers upon the earth."[6]

Then, putting his hands upon the heads of his dearly loved children, he said, "May all purchased and promised blessings be multiplied unto you!"[7]

Speaking particularly to Janet, he tenderly left her with this, "My sweet bairn, give your hand to God as your guide, and be your mother's comfort."[8]

Having heard quite enough, Claverhouse interrupted John Brown's farewells. "No more of this!" he yelled. "You six dragoons there, fire on the fanatic!"[9]

In his last moment, John declared, "Blessed be Thou, O Holy Spirit! That speaketh more comfort to my heart than the voice of my oppressors can speak terror to my heart."[10]

---

5. Ibid.

6. McGavin, *Memoirs of John Brown*, 31–36.

7. Gilfillan, *The Martyrs, Heroes and Bards*, 88–90.

8. Howie and Carslaw, *The Scots Worthies*, 442–445.

9. Gilfillan, *The Martyrs, Heroes and Bards*, 88–90.

10. McGavin, *Memoirs of John Brown*, 31–36.

But the dragoons could not bring themselves to shoot the man after hearing his fervent prayers and sweet farewells. The courageous and faithful presence of his wife and children compounded the situation. The dragoons raised their hands in protest.

Claverhouse could not tolerate this insolence. In a fit of rage, he drew his own pistol and instantly shot John in the head. Isabel caught his shattered body as he fell, embracing him as she wept.

Many years later, Isabel shared her story with Patrick Walker, a Scottish historian. Through her recollections, we know details of the family's crushing loss on that May morning. Isabel said she felt strong and of clear mind until the shot that took John's life. Her eyes, she said, then "dazled."[11]

Having killed John, Claverhouse then sarcastically demanded, "What thinkest thou of thy husband now, woman?"

"I ever thought meikel good of him, and now more than ever," Isabel bravely replied.

Appalled and angered by her honest answer but forbidden by the Privy Council to kill women through any method other than drowning, Claverhouse spat back at her, "Wretch! It were but justice to lay thee beside him."

"If ye were permitted, I doubt not but your cruelty could go that length; but how are ye to answer for this morning's wark?" Isabel challenged.

---

11. Thomson and Hutchison, *The Martyr Graves of Scotland*, 142–146.

Reeling in shock and full of his own righteousness, Claverhouse defiantly answered, "To man, I can be answerable;
and, as for God, I will take him in my own hand!"[12]

Browning and a few of the dragoons came out of the house
with "treasonable papers" and a pistol. Most likely, the con-
demning papers were nothing more nor less than a Geneva
Bible and a copy of the Westminster Confession of Faith. The
pistol, illegal for civilian use, probably served John and Isabel
upon the lonely moors at night, especially considering that
Isabel frequently remained alone with the children.

Claverhouse declared these possessions treasonous, justi-
fying his actions to himself. Young Browning expected freedom in exchange for his betrayal, but Claverhouse, holding
no respect for him, took Browning prisoner.

He then hastily climbed onto his horse and commanded
his men to leave at once. As the men sped away, Isabel lovingly set John's body down, gathered up the strewn remnants
left by the bullet's work and bound her husband's head with
her own shawl. She then pulled her children close, sat down
near his body to exclaim her heart-rending grief.

---

12. Gilfillan, *The Martyrs, Heroes and Bards of the Scottish Covenant*, 88–90.

TWELVE

WERE IT BUT JUSTICE

MILES AWAY FROM THE scene of the murder, Alexander Peden arrived at a friend's house after parting with the Browns in peace so early that morning. When he entered the home around 8:00 in the morning, Peden exclaimed, "Lord, when wilt Thou avenge Brown's blood! O, let Brown's blood be precious in Thy sight!"

His friend, John Muirhead, looked up in alarm and asked Peden what he was talking about. Peden then responded, "What do I mean? Claverhouse has been at Priesthill this morning, and has murdered John Brown. His corpse is lying at the end of his house, and his poor wife sitting weeping by his corpse, and not a soul to speak comfortably to her."

The Muirhead family pressed Peden further. How could he know this? Peden answered rapturously, "This morning, after the sun-rising, I saw a strange apparition in the firmament, the appearance of a very bright, clear, shining star fall from heaven to the earth. And indeed there is a clear, shining light fallen this day, the greatest Christian that I ever conversed with."[1]

Stunned by this declaration, the family sat mute. After a while, a neighbor Jean Brown happened by to find the little

---

1. Hewison, *The Covenanters*, 473–474.

Muirhead family all huddled together in tears. Mrs. Brown had experienced excruciating loss herself. Her husband died at the battle of Rullion Green and her sons at Drumclog. She opened her arms to the young Muirhead wife and wept with her. In response to the tragic news of Priesthill, Jean Brown assumed a commanding bearing and sent for the nearby Steel family to go and care for their dear friend Isabel.

David Steel, who once spent that sweet night of worship with John on the moors, came quickly with his wife, Mary Weir. As Mary drew near to her dear friend Isabel, she held out her arm exclaiming, "Wow, woman! And has your master been taken from your head this day? And has God taken you and your children under his own care, saying, 'I will be a husband to the widow, and a father to the fatherless?' No wonder though ye are overcome and astonished at his doings."[2]

Mary's words strengthened Isabel's spirit. The memory of all her conversations with husband John came flooding back. She remembered Peden's benediction on her wedding day, and the last words spoken between her and John. Upon these thoughts, she drew comfort and conviction of God's strength and holy plan for their lives.

David Steel's brother, William, soon arrived. The two men worked together to prepare John's body and dig a grave. While they worked, the women gathered in the house and prepared a meal. Then, before having a small service, the

---

2. McGavin, *Memoirs of John Brown*, 37–44.

small crowd of John's family and friends gathered around the table in prayer and feasting. David Steel led the group in singing a portion of Psalm 27,

> 5. For in the time of trouble he shall hide me in his Tabernacle: in the secret place of his pavilion shall he hide me, and set me up upon a rock.
> 6. And now shall he lift up mine head above mine enemies round about me: therefore will I offer in his Tabernacle sacrifices of joy: I will sing and praise the Lord. (27:5–6 1599 Geneva Version)

When David finished reading from the Scriptures, the crowd moved outside to bury John and conduct a short memorial service. They prayed and remembered their husband, father and friend.

On John's gravestone, likely erected much later,[3] they wrote,

> Here lies the body of John BROWN, Martyr, who was murdered in this place by GRAHAM of Claverhouse for his testimony to the Covenant and work of Reformation because he durst not own the authority of the then Tyrant destroying the Same, who died the first day of May AD 1685 and of his age 58.

They also inscribed this rough acrostic on the gravestone,

---

3. According to Dane Love, this gravestone was probably erected around 1700, once it was safe to do so. At the time, they probably did little more than erect a cairn of stones on the site to mark it.

In death's cold bed the dusty part here lies
    Of one who did the earth as dust despise
Here in this place from earth he took departure
    Now he has got the garland of the martyr

Butchered by Clavers and his bloody band.
    Raging most ravenously over all the land.
Only for owning Christ's supremacy
    Wickedly wronged by encroaching Tyranny.
Nothing how near soever he too good.
    Esteemed, nor dear for any truth his blood.[4]

While the Brown family mourned the death of their patriarch, Claverhouse wrote his account of the death of John Brown to the Lord Treasurer of Scotland, James Douglas, who was also the second Duke of Queensberry.[5]

3rd May 1685.

May it please your Grace,—

On Friday last, amongst the hills betwixt Douglas and the Ploughlands, we pursued two fellows a great way through the mosses, and in end seized them. They had no arms about them, and denied they had any. But being asked if they would take the abjuration, the eldest of the two, called John Brown, refused it; nor would he swear

---

4. McGavin, *Memoirs of John Brown*, 31–36.

5. John Cunningham, *The Church History of Scotland, from the Commencement of the Christian Era to the Present Century* (Edinburgh: A. & C. Black, 1859), 239–240.

not to rise in arms against the king, but said he knew no king. Upon which, and there being found bullets and match in his house, and treasonable papers, I cause shoot him dead; which he suffered very unconcernedly. The other, a young fellow and his nephew, called John Brownen, offered to take the oath, but would not swear that he had not been at Newmilns in arms, at rescuing of the prisoners. So I did not know what to do with him. I was convinced that he was guilty, but saw not how to proceed against him. Wherefore, after he had said his prayers, and carbines presented to shoot him, I offered to him that, if he would make an ingenuous confession, and make a discovery that might be of any importance for the king's service, I should delay putting him to death, and plead for him. Upon which he confessed that he was at the attack of Newmills, and that he had come straight to the house of his uncle's on Sunday morning. In the time he was making this confession, the soldiers found out a house in the hill, under ground that could hold a dozen men, and there were swords and pistols in it; and this fellow declared that they belonged to his uncle, and that he had lurked in that place ever since Bothwell, where he was in arms. He confessed that he had a halbert, and told who gave it him about a month ago, and we have the fellow prisoner. He gave an account of the most part of those that were there. They were not above sixty; and they were all Gaston and Newmills men, save a few out of Straven parish. He gave also account of a conventicle, kept by Renwick at the back of Carntable, where there were thirteen score of men in arms, mustered and exercised, of which number he was with his halbert. He tells us of another conventicle about three months ago, kept near Loudon Hill, and gives account of the persons who were at both, and what children were baptized, particularly that at Carntable, which was about the time that Lieutenants Murray and Crichton should have let them escape. He also gives account of those who gave assistance to his uncle; and we have seized thereupon the goodman of the upmost Ploughlands, and another tenant, about a mile below, that is fled. I doubt not, if we had time to stay, good use might be made of his confession. I have acquitted myself when I have told your Grace the case. He has been but a month or two with his halbert; and if your Grace thinks he deserves no mercy, justice will pass on him; for I having no commission of justiciary myself, have delivered him up to the Lieutenant-General to be disposed of as he pleases.

I am, my Lord, your Grace's most humble servant,

J. Grahame (of Claverhouse)[6]

In this letter, we see Claverhouse's view of things and we learn that John Browning desperately tried to save his own life

---

6. Andrew Murray Scott, "Letters of John Graham of Claverhouse" in *Miscellany of the Scottish History Society*, vol. 11 (Edinburgh: Scottish History Society, 1990). The original letter is preserved in Drumlanrig Castle, Dumfriesshire.

and justify John Brown's death. Young Browning even went so far as to place his uncle John at Bothwell Bridge. However, the historical record suggests otherwise. It was unlikely that John would have abandoned his wife just as she was giving birth to little Janet to take part in the Battle of Bothwell Bridge. In addition to the misinformation about John Brown, Browning's testimony possibly led to the deaths of two other people.

After taking John Browning prisoner and questioning him thoroughly, Claverhouse promised him leniency and gave him to a Captain Drummond who had him hung without hesitation.

In December of 1686, Isabel still lived at Priesthill, raising her brood of three children. As the wind blew, she heard alarming noises coming across the moors. Worried about her neighbors, Isabel took off to the Steel's home. There she found Mary weeping over David Steel's body. In a scenario much like that of John Brown's, dragoons had come across David as he worked near his home. He started to run from them but stopped when they promised not to harm him. As he turned to speak with them, they shot him.

Mary witnessed the murder from afar. When she got to his body, she said, "The archers have shot at thee, but they could not reach thy soul: it has escaped like a dove, far away, and is at rest."[7]

Isabel soon came and comforted Mary as Mary had comforted her. Isabel reminded her of her own encouraging words

---

7. McGavin, *Memoirs of John Brown*, 37–44.

to Isabel when John died. They strengthened each other as they walked through their grief.

David's gravestone has this engraved upon it:
David a shepherd first, and then
Advanced to be king of men,
Had of his graces in this quarter,
This heir, a wand'rer, now a martyr;
Who for his constancy and zeal,
Still to the back did prove good steel;
Who for Christ's royal truth and laws,
And for the covenanted cause
Of Scotland's famous Reformation,
Declining tyrant's usurpation,
By cruel Crichton murder'd lies,
Whose blood to heaven for vengeance cries.[8]

8. Ibid.

THIRTEEN

The Revolution Settlement

After John's death, the Covenanters faced three more years of dark tribulation in Scotland. During this time, Renwick and Peden hid from the authorities, travelled and preached to the best of their abilities. More cruel martyrdoms took place throughout the country.

After killing John Brown, Claverhouse continued to seek out renegade Covenanters throughout the countryside. His superior Sir James Johnstone of Westerhall, heard about an older lady who sheltered and buried a dying Covenanter. Her sons helped her dig the grave. During this time of the struggle, the authorities forbid even give a glass of water to a Covenanter. Enraged by this harboring act toward a dying man, Johnstone sent soldiers to raze her house. Westerhall dispatched Claverhouse to find her sons. He found only one, Andrew Hislop.

Claverhouse arrested Andrew Hislop and took him to Westerhall on May 10, 1685. Johnstone judged him to be guilty of being a Covenanter and ordered Claverhouse to execute him on May 11. Claverhouse uncharacteristically hesitated to carry out the execution. He declared to his superior, "The blood of this poor man be upon you, Westerhall. I am free of it." Finally, Claverhouse ordered Andrew Hislop's execution. His Highlander infantry refused, but his dragoons carried out the sentence.[1]

Why had Claverhouse hesitated? Was he perhaps plagued with guilt over his brutal murder of John Brown? A relative of Claverhouse's wife,[2] Jean, the Viscountess of Dundee, remembered Claverhouse confessing that "Brown's dying prayer could never be effaced from his executioner's memory."[3]

On May 11, 1685, just ten days after John Brown's cruel death, another hideous martyrdom of the Covenanters took place. Three women went to trial for adhering to their Presbyterian faith in Wigtown. Margaret McLauchlan, a lady of about sixty years of age, frequently led her family in worship and encouraged others to seek Christ as well. Word of her devotion made its way to the officials, and they sent the soldiers to ask her to take the Abjuration Oath. When she refused, they took her into custody.

Margaret and Agnes Wilson, sisters aged 18 and 13 respectively, fled from their parents' Wigtown home with their brother to practice their beliefs. While in hiding among the caves in the moors, the two girls heard talk that the soldiers had stopped looking for them and decided to try to sneak into town for a time to see their parents. When Margaret and Agnes sneaked into town, they were soon found out and arrested. Their parents managed only to protect the younger daughter, but not Margaret.

---

1. Hewison, *The Covenanters*, 478–479.

2. Her cousin was John Cochrane of Waterside.

3. Hewison, *The Covenanters*, 474.

Though far from being more humane than the quick death by bullets, the Scottish state limited capital punishment of women to drowning. The executioners thus tied the two Margarets to stakes in the Solway Firth (estuary) leaving them to the slowly rising tide. Robert Grierson Lag, Claverhouse's close friend, supervised the ordeal and ordered his soldiers to strategically place the older woman further out into the water so that when she was drowning, they could try to get the younger Margaret to take the Abjuration Oath.

As the tide began to drown Margaret McLauchlan, the soldiers ordered Margaret Wilson to watch and asked her what she saw. "What do I see? Christ and his members wrestling there. Think you we are the sufferers? No! It is Christ in us; for he sends none a warfare on their own charges," Margaret Wilson boldly replied.[4]

She then began to sing Psalm 25, recited Romans 8 and then prayed. The water began to cover her as she prayed. Not willing to see the young girl die just yet, Lag ordered the soldiers to bring her back in and ask if she would pray for the king. Her family and friends assembled there and pleaded with her to pray and say, "God save the King." She resolutely replied, "God save him if He will; it is his salvation I desire!"

Lag responded with a few choice words and shouted, "We do not want such prayers—tender the oaths to her!" She refused and rather than tying her back up, the soldiers held

---

4. Purves, *Sweet Believing*, 54.

her under the water until she drowned.[5]

As James II continued his reign over Scotland (1685–1688), he sought to eradicate the Covenanters and return the Scottish people to the Roman Catholic tradition. He received moral and financial support in this mission from Louis XIV of France, who successfully crushed the Protestant French Huguenot rebellion in his own country. James's violent actions prompted several plots to remove him from his throne, but only one, in 1685, showed significant promise.

Accused of treason for being lukewarm in his support of the Test Act, Archibald the Earl of Argyll fled Scotland in 1681. This Act required anyone in a public office to declare allegiance to the Episcopal Church alone. His fleeing for asylum astonished most Scots as Argyll had long supported the government. He sought refuge in Holland during the intervening years and grew more convicted in his faith. As he and his fellow exiles studied the situation in Scotland and England, they grew bold to plan a coup d'état. Argyll sailed from Holland on May 2, 1685, with every intention of uniting the Covenanters against James II's government. However, before he landed, James and the Privy Council learned of his plans to overthrow the crown in Scotland. Soon after Argyll landed, once more government forces captured him and his fellow conspirators.

Argyll went to his execution on June 30, 1685. Macauley records that when he went to the scaffold, an Episcopal clergyman called out, "My Lord dies a Protestant." To this

---

5. Ibid., 56.

Argyll added, "Yes, and not only a Protestant, but with a heart hatred of Popery, of Prelacy, and of all superstition."[6]

The authorities imprisoned nearly 200 of Argyll's men in Dunnottar Castle. Those soldiers who survived their time at Dunnottar Castle and refused to take the Abjuration Oath, the authorities bound into slavery among the colonial British plantations on the Caribbean and in America.

Following this success, in June of 1685, Claverhouse received promotion to Brigadier. He made it his next personal mission to find and execute Covenanter leader and pastor James Renwick. Renwick was growing ever more annoying to the government.

Renwick's life as a vagabond preacher put great strain on his already weak constitution. Nonetheless, he pushed himself and travelled throughout Scotland, as the sole minister and leader of the Covenanters.

On May 28, 1685, following in the footsteps of Cameron and Cargill, Renwick posted a second Sanquhar Declaration at the Market Cross in Sanquhar with a group of 200 Covenanter men in support. This Declaration denounced James II as a murderer and idolater. If anything, this act drew a deeper line in the sand between Renwick and the Scottish authorities.

During the summer of 1685, the Scots Parliament met to execute several acts of legislation against the Covenanters. Parliament raised a standing army and a tax to support

---

6. W. H. Carslaw, *Life and Letters of James Renwick, the Last Scottish Martyr* (London: Oliphant, Anderson and Ferrier, 1893), 118.

it. Husbands now incurred fines for wives absent from the church rolls. King James continued, with slow but steady progress, to maneuver the Privy Council in Scotland and the English Parliament toward Roman Catholic laws. He used his royal influence and power to fill both Parliaments with supporters, ensuring the passage of his authoritarian laws.

Alexander Peden continued his nomadic existence in Scotland, wandering throughout the countryside leading conventicles. He found shelter in the caves and in the homes of faithful friends. In 1686, at sixty years of age, Peden fell ill in a "hidie-hole" he kept as a home. Realizing death came upon him, he sent for James Renwick.[7]

This request appears strange. For years, Peden was suspicious of Renwick's doctrine and actually denounced him. He appeared just too independent. Nonetheless, Renwick went to Peden's deathbed. Peden looked Renwick up and down, saying, "I think your legs too small, and your shoulders too narrow, to take on the whole Church of Scotland on your back. Sit down, sir, and give me an account of your conversion, and of your call to the ministry, of your principles, and the grounds of your taking such singular courses, in withdrawing from all other ministers."[8]

Peden then quizzed Renwick on his beliefs and experience. In the end, Peden recognized Renwick's dedication to

---

7. Hewison, *The Covenanters*, 500.

8. Patrick Walker, *Six Saints of the Covenant in Two Volumes* (London: Hodder and Stoughton, 1901), 107–108.

Christ and His Word. Peden apologized for his unfair judgment saying, "Ye have answered me to my soul's satisfaction, and I am very sorry that I should have believed any such ill reports of you, which have not only quenched my love to you, and marred my sympathy with you, but have made me express myself too bitterly against you, for which I have sadly smarted. But, sir, ere you go you must pray for me, for I am old, and going to leave the world. . . . Sir, I find you a faithful servant to your Master. Go on in a singular dependence on the Lord, and ye shall win honestly through and cleanly off the stage."[9] With the blessing of Peden, Renwick then went on his way and continued his ministry.

As Peden lay dying he predicted that his body would be desecrated: "I shall be decently buried by you; but if my body be suffered to rest in the grave where you shall lay it, then I have been a deceiver, and the Lord hath not spoken by me: whereas, if the enemy come a little afterwards to take it up and carry it away to bury it in an ignominious place, then I hope you will believe that God Almighty hath spoken by me, and consequently there shall not one word fall to the ground."[10]

On January 26, Peden died a natural death in the company of family and friends. His brother buried him in the Auchinleck churchyard. Miraculously, after one prison sen-

---

9. Alexander Smellie, *Men of the Covenant*, 10th ed. (London, England: Banner of Truth Trust, 1960). 468–469.

10. Cameron, *Peden the Prophet*, 29.

tence and a twenty-year struggle against the government, Peden remained a free man to his death.

Remarkably, his words became reality when the Privy Council heard that Peden had died. They dug up his body and hanged it in the town of Cumnock for all to see. After a few days of this morbid and arrogant display, soldiers buried him once more, this time at the foot of the gallows, to dishonor and humiliate his memory. In response, about fifty years later, the townspeople made the gallows their new community grave yard and thus gave dignity and honor to auld Sandy Peden's legacy.

By February of 1687, King James II began to relent from his intense persecution, granting a general pardon to the Scottish people. Presbyterians may now practice their faith within their own homes, but they still could only attend services performed by approved ministers. At the same time, James repealed all laws against Catholicism thus allowing it to take root in Scotland and England.

Although King James II lessened his persecution of the Covenanters, he still sought to undermine the ministry of Renwick. Rumors spread that Renwick's ordination was invalid and that he was a notorious heretic. Renwick responded to these claims in March of 1687 by publishing *An Informatory Vindication of a Poor Wasted Misrepresented Remnant of the Suffering Anti-Popish Anti-Prelatic Anti-Erastian Anti-Sectarian True Presbyterian Church of Christ in Scotland United Together in General Correspondence. By Way of Reply to Various Accusations in Letters Informations and Conference*

Given Forth Against Them. This refutation restored Renwick's reputation as a faithful Covenanter.

By the end of 1687, there had been 13 intensive searches for Renwick throughout the country and he had managed to escape them all. However, his luck began to run out in January, 1688. Renwick had been preaching in and around Edinburgh and attracted the attention of the local authorities. On February 1, authorities arrested Renwick at a friend's house in Edinburgh. His offense? He denied the King's authority and encouraged the Covenanters to defend themselves against persecution. When questioned on the charge of denying the king's authority, he famously declared:

> I own all authority which has its prescription and limitation from the Word of God, but cannot own this usurper as lawful king, seeing both by the Word of God such a one is incapable to bear rule, and also by the ancient laws of the kingdom, which admit none to the Crown of Scotland until he swear to defend the Protestant religion, and which a man of his profession cannot do.[11]

Renwick faced trial and was found guilty of all charges. Wanting to rid themselves of this leader quickly, the judge had him hung on the scaffold at the Grassmarket in Edinburgh on February 17, 1688. The night before, a Covenanter managed to sneak into his cell and gave Renwick a chance to write his testimony. It is as follows:

---

11. Purves, *Sweet Believing*, 79

He has strengthened me to brave man and face death, and I am now longing for the joyful hour of my dissolution, and there is nothing in the world that I am sorry to leave but you; but I go to better company, and so I must take my leave of you all. Farewell beloved sufferers, and followers of the Lamb; farewell Christian intimates; farewell Christian and comfortable Mother and Sisters; farewell sweet societies; farewell desirable general meetings; farewell night wanderings in cold and weariness for Christ; farewell sweet Bible and preaching of the Gospel; farewell sun, moon and stars, and all sublunary things; farewell conflicts with a body of sin and death. Welcome scaffold for Precious Christ; welcome heavenly Jerusalem; welcome innumerable company of angels; welcome general assembly and church of the first born; welcome crown of glory, white robes and songs of Moses and the Lamb, and above all, Welcome, O Thou blessed Trinity and one God! O eternal One! I commit my soul into Thy eternal rest."[12]

Renwick was twenty-six years old. On his last day, he was allowed him to write a last letter to his faithful friend and mentor residing in Holland, Robert Hamilton. It read in part:

Right hon. and dear Sir,
This being my last day upon earth, I thought it my duty to send you this my last salutation. The Lord hath

---

12. Ibid., 82.

been wonderfully gracious to me since I came to prison, He hath assured me of His salvation, helped me to give a testimony for Him, and own before his enemies all that I have taught, and strengthened me to resist and repel many temptations and assaults. O! praise to His name . . .

Remember me to all that are friends to you, particularly to the Ladies at Lewarden, to whom I would have written, if I had not been kept close in prison, and pen, ink, and paper kept from me. But I must break off. I go to your God and my God. Death to me is as a bed to the weary. Now, be not anxious; the Lord will maintain His cause and own His people. He will show His glory yet in Scotland. Farewell, beloved and comfortable Sir. Sic subscribitur, James Renwick[13]

Several months after the death of Renwick, in July of 1688, came the fall of the last Covenanter martyr. George Wood, a young boy of sixteen, walked about his village of Sorn when *tryper* (trooper) John Reid saw him. Reid knew Wood to be a Covenanter. Reid treacherously approached without a word and murdered him. Wood's family buried him in the

---

13. James Renwick and Thomas Houston. *Spiritual Support and Consolation in Difficult Times: The Letters of the Rev. James Renwick, the Last of Scotland's Covenanted Martyrs, with an Introduction Containing a Historical Sketch of Renwick's Life, Labours, and Martyrdom, and a Vindication of His Character and Testimony* (Paisley, Scotland: Alex. Gardner, 1865), 285–286. Emphases added.

local church graveyard with a gravestone saying, "Here lyes George Wood who was shot at Tinkhornhill by bloody John Reid Tryper for his adherence to the Word of God and the Covenanted Work of Reformation, 1688."[14]

Adding to all the murderous grief of those days, all hope for the Covenanter cause appeared lost when on June 10, 1688, the wife of King James II of England and VII of Scotland bore him a son. Few could doubt the heir to the throne would be a staunch Catholic.

But then the exiled Scottish nobles in Holland began to stir with a plot to overthrow James's dynasty. Energy swirled around King James' daughter Mary, a devout Protestant. Mary was married to the Protestant leader of Holland, William of Orange. In October of 1688, William penned a Declaration against James. This Declaration strongly defended Covenanter beliefs, accusing James of merciless persecution. William also defended the right of his wife, Mary, to rule England and Scotland.[15] This was the beginning of the Glorious or Bloodless Revolution (1688–1689).[16]

---

14. A. Sinclair Horne and Eileen Dunkerley, *The Scottish Covenanters Under Persecution: 300 Years Ago Was "The Killing Time"* (Asheville, NC: The Presbyterian Journal, Oct. 35, 1985).

15. For background on William and Mary, see: John van der Kiste, *William and Mary: Heroes of the Glorious Revolution* (Stroud, UK: History Press, 2008); Henri and Barbara Van der Zee, *William and Mary* (New York: Knopf, 1973).

16. See Mary-Elaine Swanson, *John Locke: Philosopher of the American Revolution* (Ventura, CA: Nordskog Publishing, 2011), for more information

With this Declaration in play, the Covenanters eagerly rose in support. Sensing a reverse in the tide, the Scottish Privy Council slyly removed the evidence of their heightened cruelty and made a show of support toward the Covenanters.

William raised an army and landed in England on November 5 and made his way to London by December 18. The overwhelming support of William's efforts persuaded King James II that the better part of wisdom would have him flee England. He never returned to England.

Throughout December of 1688 and the early months of 1689, the Rabbling of the Curates took place.[17] The target was those clerics who had conspired with King James against the consciences of the Covenanters, leading to their persecution. In this *rabbling*, the Scots expelled them out of their churches, and publicly disgraced them in the town squares.

In January of 1689, the English Parliament officially renounced James' connection to the throne and recognized William and Mary as joint sovereigns. This marked the beginning of a new practice. Now through the representation of Parliament, the people would approve or disapprove claims to the throne, rather than passively accept the pretension of a *Divine Right* to the succession of the throne. Upon selecting William and Mary as reigning monarchs another new thing appeared. Now rather than establish a prevailing established particular church, William and the English Par-

---

on Locke and the philosophical background of the Glorious Revolution.

17. A *rabbling* is the act of a rabble or mob.

liament passed sweeping legislation affirming religious toleration of Christian denominations.

Claverhouse refused loyalty to William and Mary. Authorities under the new king and queen permitted him to leave England and return to his property in Scotland—a generous act considering the murderous persecution he had lately perpetrated on his neighbors. Soon after his return to Scotland, Claverhouse began to work toward the restoration of King James II to the throne. This attempt failed miserably, resulting in the authorities to publicly denounce several high ranking Scottish officials, including Claverhouse, and to declare them rebels.

Soon after, the Estates followed the English Parliament's example and confirmed William and Mary as sovereigns over Scotland on April 11, 1689. Nonetheless, Claverhouse, still determined to fight for the Stuart monarchy, raised an army of 2500 men to challenge the Scots in the Highlands at Killiecrankie. General Mackay led 4,200 troops against Claverhouse. Impatient with the course of the battle, Claverhouse commanded his men to charge, and as they rode forward Mackay shot Claverhouse through his head, immediately ending the life of this singular man of history on the battlefield at Killiecrankie.

Ironically, the battle ended in victory for Claverhouse's rebels. In response, the Scottish Cameronian Regiment, composed almost entirely of Covenanters, made their way to Killiecrankie. Accounts of the day speak of their singing Psalms and encouraging one another to push forward. Eventually, the last of the rebel army surrendered. The regiment went on to become famous within the Scottish army as the 26th Foot, the Cameronians.

On April 15, 1690, the second session of William and Mary's first Scots Parliament convened. Parliament reinstated the Westminster Confession of Faith and Presbyterian Church order. Parliament also provided for a General Assembly in October of 1690, the first in thirty-nine years.

The Covenanters finally won the right to worship freely as Presbyterians. However, the state still controlled much of the church, even legislating General Assembly. The battles suggested by this continued arbitrary authority would yet come. Yet already the martyrs' blood effectively sang out from the earth for justice and liberty, vindicated in its shedding and righteous in its purpose.

> They were easily defeated, and mercilessly punished; but neither defeat nor punishment could subdue their spirit. Hunted down like wild beasts, tortured till their bones were beaten flat, imprisoned by hundreds, hanged by scores, exposed at one time to the license of soldiers from England, abandoned at another time to the mercy of troops of marauders from the Highlands, they still stood at bay in a mood so savage that the boldest and mightiest oppressor could not but dread the audacity of their despair.[18]

---

18. R. Lawson, *The Covenanters of Ayrshire: Historical and Biographical* (Paisley: J. & R. Parlane, 1887), 52.

FOURTEEN

A COVENANTED NATION— GOING DEEPER

JOHN BROWN COMMITTED HIS sojourn on earth not to ease and self-interest but to a much greater cause. In this, he played a small but significant part in historic drama. To fully comprehend the magnitude and significance of John Brown's life, his time, and his and others' sacrifices, we must consider the events that produced the Covenanter Movement.[1] In turn, the Covenanter Movement, a relatively local series of events, contributed to the greater one forwarding a general liberty. The Covenanter love of liberty contributed to the notion and reality of a free and independent America. Eventually it contributed to a worldwide taste for liberty. In part, John Brown's and the Covenanter and Presbyterian stories serve to illustrate that true liberty comes only by the hand of God and only with a commitment to faith and steadfastness by God's people.

---

1. This section offers a deeper discussion for the serious Christian. It reveals the great and universal struggle of sinful men. With myriad clever devices, Godless men constantly oppose those who seek to worship the Living God on His terms, to live self-consciously for Him in all areas of life—to take every thought captive to the obedience of Christ, for His glory (2 Corinthians 10:5).

The Covenanters did not explode into a sudden flame, but rather their flame resulted from a long, slow kindling. Over centuries, Reformed Protestants faced oppression and encroachment upon all their most basic religious liberties. For Europe, great highs and tremendous lows filled the period of 1300 to 1500. John Wycliffe and others began to restore a Biblical life view to counter the corruption of the Roman Church. The parallel and overlapping Renaissance (re-birth) of Classical Greek and Roman thinking bloomed with great advances in art, engineering and exploration.[2] But, also, in the backdrop raged virulent plagues, power struggles, and political oppression.

While the Renaissance flourished in a full swing, a great struggle of ideas took place. Here it is important to note how the medieval Catholic Church varied vastly from the current institution. The Church now ruled, fought wars and conquered land. It was not simply a place of worship, it became a religious monarchy with great political power. The religious and political struggle became more pronounced as the Black Plague swept through Europe and the Catholic Church

---

2. Great movements are rarely pure. History largely views the Renaissance as a secular and humanistic intellectual movement, while many Christians would argue that whatever positive results came from the Renaissance, they mostly grew out of the restored Biblical idea of God and Man, with its view individual human value and contribution, and Christian of liberty. We argue that, as often happens, secularists co-opted this historic move of God which should have been for His glory. God always has a providential answer to such humanistic opposition. — editor.

entered into power struggles against civil monarchies. Not all effects of this struggle were negative. Many Christians began to view religion, theology and the church in a different and better light, though often with confusion along the way.

The Roman Church entrenched its power, in part, by restricting access to the Bible. At that point in history, only priests and higher clerics had access to the Bible, and only in the Latin Vulgate. The Roman Church delivered sermons only in Latin. For all practical purposes, the Church kept the Bible and its wealth of understanding out of the reach of the common man and woman. This meant that the institutional church held enormous power over the souls of the people, and therefore over their ordinary earthly lives as well.

The Church also extended its power and influence by extending the traditional sacrament of penance to the dead in purgatory. In 1460, the people could buy *indulgences* on behalf of loved ones suffering in the fires of purgatory for their temporal sins. By purchasing an indulgence for loved ones, people could supposedly reduce their suffering.[3]

Lastly, the church held full power over the destination of the soul. If the Roman Church did not forgive, God did not forgive. Separation from the church meant separation from livelihood and any possible help from family or neighbors. Excommunication could supposedly cost one's eternal life, and certainly could cost one's earthly life.

---

3. John D. Woodbridge and Frank A. James. *Church History*, vol. 2 (Grand Rapids, MI: Zondervan, 2013), 114.

No one realized it at the time, but Johannes Gutenberg, the inventor of the reusable-type printing press in the 1450s, would change the world. With this innovation, the Bible suddenly became accessible. The tide for Christians and for the Roman Church soon would begin to flow differently.

John Wycliffe completed the first English translation of the Bible in 1382. In response to his calls for reform, he suffered recrimination and lost his teaching position at Oxford University. Such was the animosity of the Church toward Wycliffe, a later pope ordered his body exhumed and burned, along with his books, forty-four years after his death.

In addition to his English Bible translation, Wycliffe also inspired a movement of itinerant lay preachers called the Lollards.[4] The Lollardy movement marked an early reform movement committed to the authority of the Bible in England prior to the Protestant Reformation. Thus, history knows Wycliffe as the *Morning Star of the Reformation*. The Lollards openly disagreed with many of the Catholic Church's teaching, transubstantiation in particular.[5] The Lollards taught literate English to the poorest citizens, spread copies

---

4. Opponents of Wycliffe called his followers *lollards* as an insult, meaning *lazy people*, because rather than work at ordinary employment, they wandered about in poverty *preaching and teaching*. As with the very name *Christian*, the Lollards took the insult upon themselves as a badge of honor and identity.

5. Transubstantiation is the belief that during communion a miracle takes place in which parishioners partake of Christ's actual body and blood.

of Wycliffe's Bible throughout the villages of England, and taught its meaning. They intended primarily to educate the people away from misleading Roman Catholic teaching, and toward a better, faith-based, and life-building Biblical way. The institutional Church quickly attempted to quash this movement, which forced the Lollards underground. Lollard preachers suffered the consequences for their opposition to the medieval Church. In Scotland, the first Lollard martyrdom occurred in 1407. Nonetheless, the Lollards' influence continued over seventy years or so until the English Reformation diffused the movement, and it died out.[6]

At the same time, the Great Schism of the Catholic Church took place. During a strategic move by the French to secure the papacy and bolster itself politically, things went wrong and two popes came into play. This confused state lasted nearly 40 years. With competing leadership, this two-headed monster led to confusion and further corruption within the institution. In 1417, the schism formally healed, but a powerful new idea (for this age) had already established itself within the Roman Church.

A conciliar movement arose in the face of rival claims to the papal throne. A decree of the Council of Constance released on April 6, 1414, made the bold assertion that "all men, of every rank and position including even the pope himself, are bound to obey [the Council] in matters that pertain to the faith, the extirpation of the said schism, and the reformation

---

6. Woodbridge and James, *Church History*, 219–220.

of the said Church in head and members."[7] This conciliar assertion served as a crack in the armor of the widely held belief that the pope was not subject to any earthly authority. While this standard did not long hold in Europe, it planted a seed of doubt in a long and closely held belief among many Christians regarding the pope's divine appointment. In Europe, times were rapidly changing.

While the Catholic Church politically weakened under its internal turmoil and power struggles, the Renaissance swept through Europe. Scholars exhumed the writings of Roman classicalists with their philosophies and musings penned during the eleventh, twelfth, and thirteenth centuries. However, interpretations of this return to classical writing and the skill of structuring arguments differed, leading to diverse conclusions. For Christians, this represented a new intellectual turn in the understanding of religion, while secularly minded humanists began to come into their own, celebrating man's achievements.[8] At a critical juncture, the German monk Martin Luther inadvertently launched the Protestant Reformation—merely by questioning the validity of Roman Church practices. The turning point occurred on October 31, 1517, when Luther posted his Ninety-Five Theses on the door of the Wittenberg church, which opposed the sale of indulgences. Forced upon him by papal pressure to recant, Luther's criticism extended over time, beyond indulgences,

---

7. Woodbridge and James, *Church History*, 45.
8. Ibid., 86.

to the very nature of salvation. For Luther and the Protestants, no one can earn salvation through works or money, but through faith in Christ alone. Over time, this concept would prove vital to the Protestant movement as it not only caused people to think deeply about their faith, but also contributed to rethinking of the meaning of and the relationships between the upper and lower classes. No longer could mere wealth or social position serve as a comfort to sinners that God somehow favored them. Rather, the work of Christ must renew the inner man—with the result of godly outgoing faith, character, and desire to serve God with courageous accomplishment. The effect was a great leveling and outgoing impetus of faith to the greater population.[9] Again, the Biblical idea of God and man began to emerge once more.

The Protestant Reformation then received an unexpected boost from a disgruntled Catholic. In England, King Henry VIII sought annulment of his marriage to his first wife Catherine, but the Church refused. Headstrong in his desire to marry the alluring Anne Boleyn and produce a male heir, Henry VIII decided to separate from the Catholic Church to form his own—the Church of England—in 1534. The churches remained in almost the same set of beliefs, with the exception that the Church of England (now also called *Anglican* or *Episcopalian*) allowed divorce. This paved the way for the English Reformation—a first step in separating from the established Roman Catholic Church and accepting true

9. Ibid., 114.

Protestantism. King Henry's son, Edward VI succeeded his father in 1547 and introduced full-fledged Protestantism to England. His sister Elizabeth I continued the Reformation of the English Church.

What is Reformation? John Calvin, born in 1509, penned the first edition of *The Institutes of the Christian Religion* in 1536 largely defining the *Reformed* view of the Christian faith. This book served as a benchmark for the Reformation and as a guide for the establishment of Protestant theology. From this work and others, Reformed Protestants derived their stances on Scripture, the sacraments, prayer, Christian life, and even civil government. From the city of Geneva, Switzerland, Calvin supported reform movements throughout Europe and especially in France. Calvin deeply influenced the Geneva Bible, published in 1557 (New Testament) and 1560 (Old Testament). It was essentially a revision of William Tyndale's English language Bible, and later became the basis of the venerable and beloved King James Version. Many future leaders of the Protestant Reformation spent time in Geneva, learning from Calvin. Among the most notable was the Covenanters' founding intellect and spiritual leader John Knox. Knox also contributed to annotative comments found in the Geneva Bible.

While the English Reformation gained hold, Scotland experienced turmoil and confusion as the Catholic Church attempted to hold and strengthen power over that country. In 1526, Patrick Hamilton, a young man of distinguished parentage, visited Martin Luther in Germany. Upon his return, he began to minister to the Scottish people from the Bible— ordinarily withheld from the people—and to preach against the Catholic Church's doctrines and policies. On February 28, 1528, James Beaton, Archbishop of St. Andrews, condemned Hamilton to death and ordered him burned at the stake. The Church subsequently caused the martyrdom of many others. Such proceedings came to a head in 1544 when a young man, George Wishart, was martyred for attempting to teach Protestant doctrines as well as the Greek language. This event proved incendiary for the Scottish people, and the Scottish Reformation began to take root.

On the heels of Wishart's martyrdom, John Knox (1515–1572) led the Scottish people in the establishment of the Presbyterian Church. Knox is known for his staunchness of faith and his refusal to cower on matters he deemed important. He stood against the Catholic Church by defiantly calling out its actions as those of the "Antichrist."[10] In so doing, he drew the line between a Biblical faith and corrupt religion. Knox called for the establishment of a new church based solely on Scripture. Knox suffered the consequences of this action. The government sentenced him to serve as a galley slave in France for two years (1547–1549). He then went to England and began to preach there as well, eventually even serving as a chaplain in the court of Edward VI.

After the youthful king Edward died and during the reign of Mary Tudor, John Knox resided in Geneva, studying with

---

10. See 1 John 2:18, 22; 4:3; 2 John 7.

Calvin. In 1559, he returned to Scotland and once again took up the cause of establishing a new church. When challenged at trial by the Catholic clergy, the people so well supported him that the court dismissed the trial, out of fear by the Roman clergy of recrimination and vengeance. Knox, taking advantage of his popularity, then spent four days preaching against popery. The people eagerly received his words, so that they redoubled their efforts to establish the new church.

Knox made himself a thorn in the side of Mary, Queen of Scots. Mary was another in a long line of Scottish royalty known as the House of Stuart (originally Stewart) hearkening back to King Robert II in the fourteenth century. The House of Stuart would continue on the throne of England through the reign of James II. Mary Stuart, the child queen, grew up a staunch Catholic and attempted to reestablish Catholicism in Scotland. Mary became the Queen of France during her short marriage to Francis II, who died young. On her return to Scotland and the throne, Mary advocated for the Catholic Church in secret and attempted to regain Scotland for the papacy. However, she found that Knox's influence had grown within the country. The Presbyterians and her own poor decisions eventually forced her from the throne. She attempted to seek shelter in England, but her English cousin Queen Elizabeth I came to execute her upon discovery of her conspiracies to overthrow the English queen.

The Scots Parliament abolished Catholicism in 1560. When James VI, son of Mary, Queen of Scots, grew old enough to fight back against the Scottish nobles and leaders, he began to advocate for Episcopal hierarchy[11] in Scotland. The root of this desire was James' belief in the divine right of kings. This concept would prove to be the primary dividing point between episcopacy and Presbyterianism. The Presbyterians recognized no king but Jesus and saw the king of the land simply as the conservator whose power has been endowed by the people and could be taken away by the people. The long-dominant theory among the Catholic Church and the royals was that kings were divinely appointed by God. In effect, to oppose the monarch was tantamount to opposing God.

James, under the influence of papists, called for a supposedly "anti-papal covenant," drafted and signed in 1581. While the document clearly reads as a pro-Bible and anti-Roman statement, James may have used it as a ruse to lull the Covenanters into complacency. James may never have intended to honor his Negative Confession or King's Confession, as it is known. Whether the Negative Confession intended deception or the king changed his thinking, this would be the first in a series of covenants agreed upon by the monarchy in practice used to appease and hoodwink the earnest Scottish Covenanters. King James finally revealed his ultimate motive when he secured enough trust from the people, gathering support in Parliament to pass the "Black Acts" on May 22, 1584. These acts declared all anti-Anglican acts of the General Assembly to be treason and upheld the king's divine right.

---

11. A vertical authority structure of ruling clerics in the church. This idea is unknown in Scriptures.

It also forbade the General Assembly to meet without royal consent.

Tensions simmered below the surface for the next few years as the Scottish Presbyterians gathered support. In 1592, James's hold on power in Scotland reached its lowest point. Seizing the opportunity, Presbyterian leaders struck back through the Parliamentary act entitled "The Ratification of Liberties of the True Church." James agreed to most of their terms and ratified the act. This meant the reestablishment of Presbyterian Church government and the repeal of the "Black Acts."

The Presbyterian view of church government prescribed a multi-tiered organization that functions at four levels starting with the local and extending geographically outward. These levels are Session, Presbytery, Synod and General Assembly. Each Presbyterian Church has a Session, which consists of elected elders who serve limited terms. The Session sends a representative to Presbytery, the regional ruling organization. The Presbytery largely provides oversight of the churches. The Presbytery reports to the Synod, which is a larger regional organization that decides upon broader issues. All of the more local assemblies report to the General Assembly, composed of representatives from all tiers. The General Assembly meets annually.

In 1603, Elizabeth I died, leaving no heirs. James VI of Scotland became James I, King of England, Scotland, and Ireland. Thus, he united the three kingdoms under one rule.

King James called for a new version of the Bible—the Authorized or King James Bible—published in 1611. Many were calling for a more accurate translation. James convened forty-six experts to translate from the original languages. King James intended his new version to replace the Geneva Bible, which was heavily annotated with anti-royalty sentiment. Tellingly, since James commissioned this translation, there is an undue emphasis on royalty and the rights of kings throughout the popular and beloved King James version.

When James VI of Scotland and I of England died in 1625, his son, Charles I succeeded him. Charles I formally ruled as the head of the Protestant English Church. However, many suspected a personal loyalty to the Roman Catholic Church. His queen, Henrietta Maria of France, was a devout Catholic who encouraged him to defy the efforts of Protestants. While James I had been content to subtly manipulate and slightly modify the Scottish church to achieve his ends, Charles I acted far from subtly. He marked his ascendance to the throne with a sweeping act of Revocation of all laws since 1542. This action erased all the progress that the Scottish Presbyterians had accomplished in their attempt to establish a new form of government in representative Presbyterian terms.

During the time of the religious turmoil brought on by James and furthered by Charles, many Separatists (Pilgrims) and Puritans prepared for and began to leave England for a new *promised land* in the Americas. The King refused the Separatists either to worship according to personal conscience or to leave England! At one point, James threatened to harry the Puritans out of the land. The ruling class treated Presbyterians in England and Scotland very unkindly in those days. This forced the dissident Christians to worship in secret lest they may lose their livelihoods, homes, freedom, or their lives. While James I quietly enforced his version of the Anglican Church—under official persecution and under great financial duress and a great series of trials—the Pilgrims left England for Holland in 1607 and left Holland for America in 1620. A group of Puritans left England for America in 1630, just as Charles I's vendetta against the Protestants grew to a pitched force. As time passed, many oppressed people of Great Britain and Europe at large went to America to seek the relief of freedom and justice.

One of James' favored advisors, William Laud, had soon ingratiated himself to Charles I. Charles allowed Laud to oversee and plot the course of religion in the three kingdoms of England, Ireland, and Scotland. Laud, intensely intelligent and power hungry, longed to see the Church of England enlarge itself in power and esteem. As one writer said, he sought to see "Rome revived, without Rome's errors."[12] Already, Laud set his sights upon Scotland, noting that he felt they had no discernible religion. It would become his "holy cause" for years to come.

In 1633, when Charles finally made his way to Scotland for his coronation, he continued the spread of episcopacy by

---

12. Of course, what was wrong with Rome, in part, was its authoritarianism—seeking to use positive force to make the people and empire good, rather than as God-ordained governments ought to do, to protect individual life, liberty and property. Thus in following Rome, England could not help but follow Rome in its errors.

naming Laud Privy Councilor of Scotland. While in Scotland for his coronation, Charles took the opportunity to observe the land and analyze the effects of his earlier Act of Revocation (1625), which returned lands given to Scottish nobles since 1540 to the crown. Encouraged by the results, he convened the Scottish Parliament and aligned with key players to pass 168 bills focusing on the revocation of Presbyterianism and the reestablishment of episcopacy in that session. The Scottish government did not reject one of his proposed bills.

Upon Charles' return, he appointed Laud as Archbishop of Canterbury. When Laud assumed office, he created a new bishopric in Edinburgh and appointed his colleague and representative William Forbes to it. Laud soon began to use Scotland as a test ground for his ambitions of a national religion based in episcopacy, which would prove to be a grave misjudgment on his part. The Scottish people never have reacted well to dictators.

In 1637, Charles mandated that the Scottish people accept his Book of Canons. The Canons, put together mostly at the hand of Laud, incorporated a high church liturgy and episcopacy. Some saw it as affirming the divine rights of kings. This is an apt observation considering that the king single-handedly imposed this national religion on a people determined to walk in a Biblical Christian liberty of conscience. Under the authority of Laud, the bishops of Scotland forced the clergy to use the Canons alone. Not surprisingly, clergy and people alike reacted with vitriol and conviction.

While the grumblings occurred everywhere in Scotland, many people filed into the churches on Sunday, July 27, 1637, the date appointed for the introduction of the Canons. At St. Giles Church in Edinburgh, Jenny Geddes brought the disapproval to a head by throwing a footstool at the head of the bishop conducting a service using the Canons. The resulting riot demonstrated the fierceness of the Scottish disapproval. The Scots remember this as the inaugural event of the Covenanter struggle. Similar feelings spread throughout the country. The Scottish people began to strategize against Charles and Laud. On witnessing the fear and multiple cases of resignation of readers and clergy, the Scottish bishops decided to suspend the Canons until the people settled down.

Several nobles then formed a band against Charles, who obstinately refused to back down from his position. To widen the appeal and bring the country together against episcopacy, this band harkened back to the King's Confession of 1581, listing all the Parliamentary acts against the establishment of episcopacy. This resulted in the National Covenant of 1638. On February 28, nobles and barons of Scotland signed this document in Greyfriars churchyard in Edinburgh. Copies made their way throughout the country. The people—citizens high and low—put their names to it. A remarkable part of this event is that almost every citizen of Scotland could read, peasants and nobility alike. With the peoples' emphasis on God's Word, the people accordingly emphasized literate education throughout the country. The people had exhibited a prevalent skill in literacy for nearly four hundred years. It truly became a National Covenant, and those who subscribed to it became known as *Covenanters*.

After attempting to frighten the Covenanters into submission by threatening war, then trying to appeal intellectually by proposing a more moderate covenant, Charles withdrew his mandate for the Canons and consented to a meeting of the General Assembly. The Scottish General Assembly met in Glasgow on November 21, 1638. Apprehending the aims of the Assembly, Charles's representative published a proclamation aimed at ending the meeting. Much to his dismay, Charles's actions actually helped to raise public support for the Presbyterian cause.

The Assembly remained convened through December 20. During this time, they systematically reviewed and repudiated old legislation, methodically eradicating episcopacy from the Scottish government and church. The existing bishops came under examination and were found wanting in regards to their personal morality and commitment to the church. The Assembly condemned and repealed Charles's various initiatives. They passed one final ground-breaking piece of legislation before adjourning: They forbade pastors from holding official government posts. This effort aimed at reducing the amount of political thrust held by the church. Separating church authority from civil authority likewise became the basis of America's First Amendment, which, as with the Scots, never intended to separate Christian faith from government, but only to diffuse power. Upon dissolving the Assembly, the representatives appointed the next Assembly for July 3, 1639.

Outraged at the actions taken during the General Assembly, Charles responded by launching a military attack. Charles gathered a small army to compel the submission of the Covenanters. In response, the Covenanters flew their banner proclaiming loyalty to "Christ's Crown and Covenant" for the first time, armed themselves, and soundly defeated the English army. This short-lived "Bishops' War" resulted in embarrassment for Charles, and he consented to an Assembly on August 12, 1639, and a subsequent Parliament to ratify the acts of the Assembly.

When the Assembly met, they ratified abolishment of episcopacy. However, due to Charles's duplicity, the meeting ended quickly. Already planning a second "Bishops' War," Charles feigned agreement with the proposals of the Scottish Assembly to distract the Covenanters. Having caught wind of Charles' subterfuge, the Covenanters convened a defiant parliament in 1640 and ratified all acts of the General Assembly in 1639. The Scots raised an army and again defeated Charles in battle. Soon the Scottish army made its way through the northern parts of England.

This embarrassment forced Charles to convene the English Parliament on November 3, 1640. This was a Puritan parliament more in accord with the Scots than their own King. This session came to be known in history as the "Long Parliament." After many months of debate and struggle, the Scots prevailed and in August of 1641, the English Parliament agreed to pay 300,000 pounds in damages to Scotland. Parliament forced Charles to ratify all acts of the Scots Parliament of 1640, thereby securing the abolishment of Scottish episcopacy. While this could have been the end of the struggle, things only just began to heat up in England as the Puritan Parliament turned its attention to abolishing English episcopacy and civil war.

As the Parliament waged a successful civil war against its King, Charles fled to Scotland, where a lingering loyalty remained. The Scottish people's greatest fault, one may argue, lay in their unrelenting loyalty to the throne. While they may strenuously disagree with the actions taken by the king, a lingering conviction remained that divine providence had placed Charles on the throne. This sense may well have derived from David's deference to King Saul in the Bible (e.g., 1 Samuel 24:6). However, Charles responded to the Scots' ingenuous honor to their king with deception. He played to their sympathies, making himself appear affable and open to their demands. While he worked on the Scottish sympathies, the English Parliament cast Archbishop Laud in the Tower of London, where he would eventually die by execution in 1645. Samuel Rutherford's 1644 book, *Lex Rex*, accurately captured the political sentiment of the day and its theoretical roots in the Bible: The king is servant to the people before God, and the law is supreme ruler under Him.

In the meantime, the English Civil War raged between Charles and the English Parliament. Seizing the opportunity, the Puritan Parliament convened a General Assembly to revise the theological doctrine of the Anglican Church. They invited some of the most influential of Scottish Covenanters to participate. This Westminster Assembly convened August 2, 1643. The first act of this Assembly to agree to the *Solemn League and Covenant* between the Scots and the Puritan parliament, which reconfigured the Anglican Church with a Presbyterian polity. While the Independents forcefully argued for local congregational government alone, the Presbyterians were a powerful voice and their view prevailed.

The Westminster Assembly produced a new doctrinal statement now known as the *Westminster Confession of Faith*, which would become the foundational document for Presbyterianism the world over. The Assembly also produced two other long-lasting documents—the Larger and Shorter Catechisms—designed for lay adults and children. The Scots Parliament accepted the acts of the Westminster Assembly and used its documents, with minor corrections, for the Scottish Church as well.

The English Civil War continued to rage. This bloody war finally resulted in the defeat of King Charles. At the end of the conflict, in 1645, Charles found himself defenseless and on the run from his own people. The Puritan armies captured Charles and put him on trial for treason. The court found him guilty, and he died by execution on January 30, 1649.

Dismayed by what the Scots considered regicide and in a strange twist of fate, even at the height of Covenanter success, Scotland reached out to Charles I's son and heir Charles II. If he would sign a covenant affirming Presbyterian polity, the Scots would acknowledge his claim to the throne.

Charles II agreed to the covenant set forth by the Scottish Presbyterians. In exchange, they supported his efforts to regain the throne of his father in England. Not surprisingly, Charles II made mostly empty promises. It is in this respect that Scotland's loyalty to the monarchy became its greatest weakness. The desire for a king made them susceptible to the perversity of power.

Charles II launched an attack on England, but he was no match for Oliver Cromwell's anti-royalist army. Like his father before him, Charles II felt a round defeat, forcing him to flee to France in 1651. For the next nine years, Parliament governed Scotland, England, and Ireland without a monarch. Cromwell's armies consolidated the three countries into one.

Cromwell's power continued to grow, and eventually he became the Lord Protector of England—a king in all but name. Cromwell remained an effective ruler until his death in 1658.

Oliver Cromwell's son Richard Cromwell succeeded him. Richard turned out to be a poor leader. Soon, Charles II began to negotiate his return as king. With Richard Cromwell's failure, the English parliament did the unthinkable. They invited Charles II to return to the English throne. However much the people may have desired it, the British Isles appeared not yet ready for self-government. Then in 1660, Charles agreed to a "covenant" of sorts. He manipulated the framers of the covenant by inserting terms of moderate episcopacy. He then resumed the throne over the three kingdoms—Scotland, England, and Ireland.

In Edinburgh, on June 19, 1660, the Scots celebrated a day of Thanksgiving for Charles' restoration to the throne. The celebration did not last long. Charles appointed a Privy Council of those loyal to him, giving them enormous power to legislate in Scotland. His exercise of authority began slowly by first quietly imprisoning opponents. Finally, on August 24, the king forbade all religious meetings not approved by the throne. The Presbyterianism and liberty the Scots had fought so ardently now and once more slipped away.

In 1661, Charles II's first Scottish Parliament met. The first statute passed placed him at the head of the church as supreme ruler of the land. On January 25, 1661, Parliament repealed the National Covenant of 1638. They then instituted the Recissory Act, nullifying all legislation passed between 1641 and 1648. This act reinstituted patronages and disestablished the regular Presbyterian Church, though not the dissenting activities of the Covenanters.

Then the terror began. The government executed several Covenanter leaders without trial. The crown ordered copies of Samuel Rutherford's *Lex Rex* books burned at the scaffolds. The tide had turned and the Covenanters faced intense persecution and a complete lack of political support.

Entering this terrifying epoch of history, John Brown of Priesthill's historic personal story then began to unfold.

A Brief Bibliography for Further Reading

Ballantyne, R. M. *Hunted and Harried: A Tale of the Scottish Covenanters*. Hayward, CA: Pinnacle Press, 2017.

Cameron, Thomas. *Peden the Prophet: "Puir Auld Sandy."* Edinburgh: Blue Banner Productions, 1998.

Carslaw, W. H. *Life and Letters of James Renwick, the Last Scottish Martyr*. London: Oliphant, Anderson and Ferrier, 1893.

Cunningham, John. *The Church History of Scotland, from the Commencement of the Christian Era to the Present Century*. Edinburgh: A. & C. Black, 1859.

Gilfillan, George. *The Martyrs, Heroes and Bards of the Scottish Covenant*. London: Cockshaw, 1852.

Hewison, J. King. *The Covenanters: A History of the Church of Scotland from the Reformation to the Revolution, in Two Volumes*. Glasgow: John Smith and Son, 1913.

Howie, John, and W. H. Carslaw. *The Scots Worthies*. Edinburgh: Banner of Truth Trust, 1995.

Lawson, R. *The Covenanters of Ayrshire: Historical and Biographical*. Paisley: J. and R. Parlane, 1887.

Love, Dane. *Scottish Covenanter Stories: Tales from the Killing Times*. Castle Douglas, UK: Neil Wilson Publishers, 2014.

Lowe, Harry William. *Scottish Heroes: Tales of the Covenanters*. Whitefish, MT: Literary Licensing, 2011.

McGavin, William. *Memoirs of John Brown, of Priesthill, and the Rev. Hugh Mackail, Two Sufferers for the Cause of the Covenanted Reformation in Scotland*. 1839.

Purves, Jock. *Fair Sunshine: Character Studies of the Scottish Covenanters*. Edinburgh: Banner of Truth, 2003.

Purves, Jock. *Sweet Believing: Eight Character Studies of the Scottish Covenanters*, 2d ed. Stirling, Scotland: Stirling Tract Enterprise, 1954.

Renwick, James, and Thomas Houston. *Spiritual Support and Consolation in Difficult Times: The Letters of the Rev. James Renwick, the Last of Scotland's Covenanted Martyrs, with an Introduction Containing a Historical Sketch of Renwick's Life, Labours, and Martyrdom, and a Vindication of His*. Paisley, Scotland: Alex. Gardner, 1865.

Scott, Andrew Murray. "Letters of John Graham of Claverhouse," in *Miscellany of the Scottish History Society 11th Volume*. Edinburgh, 1990.

Smellie, Alexander. *Men of the Covenant*, 10th ed. London, England: Banner of Truth Trust, 1960.

Thomson, J. H., and Matthew Hutchison. *The Martyr Graves of Scotland*. Edinburgh: Oliphant, Anderson & Ferrier, 1903.

Van der Kiste, John. *William and Mary: Heroes of the Glorious Revolution*. Stroud, UK: History Press, 2008.

Van der Zee, Henri and Barbara. *William and Mary*. New York: Knopf, 1973.

Vos, Johannes. *The Scottish Covenanters: Their Origins, History and Distinctive Doctrines*. Edinburgh: Blue Banner Productions, 1998.

Walker, Patrick. *Six Saints of the Covenant in Two Volumes*. London: Hodder and Stoughton, 1901.

Woodbridge, John D., and Frank A. James. *Church History, vol. 2*. Grand Rapids, MI: Zondervan, 2013.

Appendix A

Timeline of Events

ca. 1300–1500s   Renaissance, a return to humanistic Greek and Roman Classicism

1382   Wycliffe's first English Bible—Morning Star of the Reformation

1387–1417   Great Western Schism of the Roman Catholic Church—multiple, competing popes

1414   Conciliar Movement—Council of Constance—makes Pope subject to other men

1440s–1450s   Gutenberg Printing Press and the Bible

1526   Scottish Patrick Hamilton visits Luther and returns to teach the Scots

ca. 1490–1527   High Renaissance humanistic art and architecture movement

1528   Archibishop of St. Andrews James Beaton burns Patrick Hamilton at the stake

1517   Martin Luther 95 Theses

1534   Henry VIII cedes from the Roman Church—beginning of the English Reformation

1536   John Calvin's *The Institutes of the Christian Religion*

1542–1567 Mary Queen of Scots reigns

1546 George Wishart martyred for teaching Protestant doctrine

1547 Elizabethan Protestantism begins

1547 John Knox begins public ministry after his time with Wishart, then exiled as a galley slave

1560 Geneva Bible

1560 John Knox declares Scotland a Presbyterian nation, and Scottish Parliament abolishes Romanism

1567–1625 James VI of Scotland, son of Mary, reigns in Scotland

1581 James makes a deceptive agreement with the Covenanters—The Negative Confession

1584 Black Acts—call all anti-Anglicanism acts of the Scottish General Assembly treason and uphold the divine right of kings

1592 Presbyterian leaders successfully pass The Ratification of Liberties of the True Church act, reestablishing Presbyterianism

1603 Elizabeth I dies and James VI became James I of England

1611 King James Version Bible

1620 Pilgrims migrate to America

1625 Death of James I, reign of King Charles I begins, and Act of Revocation reverses Presbyterian progress

1627 John Brown Birth

1630 English Puritans begin their migration to America

1633 Charles I crowned in Scotland, and with Laud pursues Episcopalianism there

1637 Charles imposes the Anglican Book of Canons on the Scots

1637 Covenanter Movement begins with the introduction of the Canons at St. Giles Church; Nobles form opposition

1638 National Covenant declares Presbyterianism for Scotland, defeats Episcopal measures

1638 Charles I temporarily permits pro-Presbyterian General Assembly meeting, then loses a military effort against the Covenanters

1640 The English Long Parliament favors the Presbyterians against Charles I and ratifies all acts of the Scots Parliament

1641 The English Civil War forces Charles to flee to Scotland

1643 Solemn League and Covenant—treaty with English Parliament to preserve Scottish Presbyterianism

1643 Westminster Assembly adopts Presbyterianism for England

1649 Charles I executed; Charles II appeals to the Scots who receive and support him

1650 Treaty of Breda, Charles II becomes King of Scotland

1651 Oliver Cromwell defeats Charles II's Scottish forces; Charles flees to France; English Parliament rules England, Ireland, Scotland for nine years

1658 Cromwell's death begins the end of the Puritan movement

1660 Parliament invites Charles II to return to the English throne; Scottish monarchy restored

1661 Rescissory Act—Charles II repeals all laws since 1633, disestablishing the Presbyterian Church and engaging terror against the Covenanters

1662 Abjuration Act—formally rejects the *National Covenant* of 1638 and *Solemn League and Covenant* of 1643

1679 Scottish Violence over Charles II policies— Assassination of Archbishop Sharp, Drumclog and the Battle of Bothwell Bridge

1680 Sanqhuar Declaration—rejects a king who did not recognize the Scottish religion

1685 Charles II died; King James VII accedes

1685 John Brown executed

1688 Last Scottish martyr, sixteen-year-old George Wood murdered

1689   English Parliament renounces James II and
       recognizes William and Mary as joint
       sovereigns

1689   The Scottish Estates confirmed William
       and Mary as Sovereigns over Scotland

1690   William and Mary's first Scots Parliament
       Convened, reinstating the Westminster
       Confession of Faith and Presbyterian
       Church order.

Appendix B

Excerpts from The Scottish National Covenant[1]

[February 37, 1638. Rushworth, ii. 734.
See Hist. of Engl viii. 329.]

THE CONFESSION OF FAITH of the Kirk of Scotland, subscribed at first by the King's Majesty and his household in the year of God 1580... by us noblemen, barons, gentlemen, burgesses, ministers, and commons under subscribing; together with our resolution and promises for the causes after specified, to maintain the said true religion, and the King's Majesty.... We all, and every one of us underwritten, do protest, that after long and due examination of our own consciences in matters of true and false religion, we are now thoroughly resolved of the truth, by the word and spirit of God; and therefore we believe with our hearts, confess with our mouths, subscribe with our hands, and constantly affirm before God and the whole world, that this only is the true Christian faith and religion, pleasing God, and bringing sal-

---

1. Source: Constitution Society, constitution.org/eng/conpur023.htm, accessed Oct. 11, 2017.

vation to man, which now is by the mercy of God revealed to the world by the preaching of the blessed evangel, and received, believed, and defended by many and sundry notable kirks and realms, but chiefly by the Kirk of Scotland, the King's Majesty, and three estates of this realm, as God's eternal truth and only ground of our salvation.... To the which confession and form of religion we willingly agree in our consciences in all points, as unto God's undoubted truth and verity, grounded only upon His written Word; and therefore we abhor and detest all contrary religion and doctrine, but chiefly all kind of papistry in general and particular heads, even as they are now damned and confuted by the Word of God and Kirk of Scotland.... To which we join ourselves willingly, in doctrine, religion, faith, discipline, and life of the holy sacraments, as lively members of the same, in Christ our head, promising and swearing, by the great name of the Lord our God, that we shall continue in the obedience of the doctrine and discipline of this Kirk, and shall defend the same according to our vocation and power all the days of our lives, under the pains contained in the law, and danger both of body and soul in the day of God's fearful judgment....

We therefore, willing to take away all suspicion of hypocrisy, and of such double dealing with God and His Kirk, protest and call the Searcher of all hearts for witness, that our minds and hearts do fully agree with this our confession, promise, oath, and subscription.... And because we perceive that the quietness and stability of our religion and Kirk doth depend upon the safety and good behaviour of the King's

Majesty . . . we protest and promise with our hearts under the same oath, hand-writ, and pains, that we shall defend his person and authority with our goods, bodies, and lives, in the defence of Christ His evangel, liberties of our country, ministration of justice, and punishment of iniquity, against all enemies within this realm or without, as we desire our God to be a strong and merciful defender to us in the day of our death, and coming of our Lord Jesus Christ; to Whom, with the Father and the Holy Spirit, be all honour and glory eternally. . . .

Like as all lieges are bound to maintain the King's Majesty's royal person and authority, the authority of Parliaments, without which neither any laws or lawful judicatories can be established, and the subjects' liberties, who ought only to live and be governed by the King's laws, the common laws of this realm allanerly which if they be innovated or prejudged the commission anent the union of the two kingdoms of Scotland and England. . . . James VI, declares such confusion would ensue as this realm could be no more a free monarchy. . . . And therefore for the preservation of the said true religion, laws and liberties of this kingdom, it is statute . . . of K. Charles, that all Kings and Princes at their coronation and reception of their princely authority, shall make their faithful promise by their solemn oath in the presence of the Eternal God, that daring the whole time of their lives they shall serve the same Eternal God to the utmost of their power, according as He hath required in His most Holy Word, contained in the Old and New Testaments, and according to the same Word shall maintain the true religion of Christ Jesus, the preaching of His Holy Word, the due and right ministration of the sacraments now received and preached within this realm (according to the confession of faith immediately preceding); and shall abolish and gainstand all false religion contrary to the same.... And finally, being convinced in our minds, and confessing with our mouths, that the present and succeeding generations in this land are bound to keep the aforesaid national oath and subscription inviolable: —

We noblemen, barons, gentlemen, burgesses, ministers, and commons under subscribing, considering divers times before, and especially at this time, the danger of the true reformed religion, of the King's honour, and of the public peace of the kingdom, by the manifold innovations and evils generally contained and particularly mentioned in our late supplications, complaints, and protestations, do hereby profess, and before God, His angels and the world, solemnly declare, that with our whole hearts we agree and resolve all the days of our life constantly to adhere unto and to defend the aforesaid true religion.... [T]hat we shall defend the same, and resist all these contrary errors and corruptions according to our vocation, and to the utmost of that power that God hath put into our hands, all the days of our life. And in like manner, with the same heart we declare before God and men, that we have no intention or desire to attempt anything that may turn to the dishonour of God or the diminution of the King's greatness and authority.... [W]e join such a life and conversation as beseemeth Christians who have renewed their covenant with God; we therefore faithfully promise, for ourselves, our followers, and all other under us, both in public, in our particular families and personal carriage, to endeavour to keep ourselves within the bounds of Christian liberty, and to be good examples to others of all godliness, soberness and righteousness, and of every duty we owe to God and man; and that this our union and conjunction may be observed without violation we call the living God, the searcher of our hearts to witness, who knoweth this to be our sincere desire and unfeigned resolution, as we shall answer to Jesus Christ in the great day, and under the pain of God's everlasting wrath, and of infamy, and of loss of all honour and respect in this world; most humbly beseeching the Lord to strengthen us by His Holy Spirit for this end, and to bless our desires and proceedings with a happy success, that religion and righteousness may flourish in the land, to the glory of God, the honour of our King, and peace and comfort of us all.

In witness whereof we have subscribed with our hands all the premises, &c.

About
WHITNEY HOBSON CRAIG

 WHITNEY HOBSON CRAIG GREW up learning about the Scottish Presbyterian tradition while she attended Emerald Mountain Christian School in Alabama, a school that specialized in understanding the lessons of Christian history toward living the Biblical faith. A life-long reader, Whitney gravitates toward biographies and seeks to understand people's place in history. She graduated from the University of Alabama with a degree in Journalism and Political Science.

Whitney currently resides in South Bend, Indiana, with her husband and son. She works as a communications specialist with a local non-profit dedicated to providing choice and possibility to people with intellectual and developmental disabilities. In her spare time, Whitney enjoys cooking, CrossFit and leading a small group for her church.

A Word from the Publisher

This book is about the modest and courageous Scottish Covenanter in the 17th century martyred for his faith in Christ and Reformed view of the Bible. He believed that view should be carried out faithfully in his life and in his family and country of Scotland during the Killing Wars of his era. He lived his life as he believed, even though his pastoral friend Alexander Peden had prophesied he would one day die a martyr for standing firm in his beliefs.

John Brown's name appeared in 1684 on the Catholic king's list of devout Christian fugitives. As one of 180 Covenanters on the list, John Brown and his close friend David Steel hid from the Royalist King's soldiers searching for him. These two men were among the many Covenanters who would not submit to the laws demanding all Scots families attend only the established royalist church. This meant government soldiers would likely hunt down and murder anyone who did not attend government services. One night while hiding in a cave, Steel and Brown, after a lengthy time of worship and prayer, read from their Bibles and sang psalms. The next morning, they heard the sweet sound of a voice singing:

> O let the prisoners' sighs ascend
> Before Thy sigh on high;
> Preserve those by Thy mighty power
> That are design'd to die

But they could not find the singer. The Covenanter friends became convinced that song was a special sign of God's favor in this time of trials. This encouraged them greatly. Brown and his wife and children lived on the farm known as Priesthill. He was well respected and loved for his Christian hospitality. John Brown held the trusted vocation of itinerant consignment trader and so became known as "The Christian Carrier of Priesthill."

This strong Christian, gentle, kind and courageous, a dedicated and faithful *believer in the Bible*, sold out in obedience to serve his Master Jesus, should be emulated today in Scotland, and in America. Where have the John Browns of Priesthill gone in our societies? Secular humanism and the lack of faith and obedience to the Word of God (even among many Christians) has expanded and infected the cultures of these two great nations—and much of the world.

We should be emulating and improving upon the Scottish Covenanters legacy, and their counterparts the American Pilgrims and Puritans. Rather, we appear relatively impotent since we have left action in the important spheres of life to the humanists and false religions in our lands. Pointedly, *we need spiritual truth and revivals in Scotland and in America. Desperately!*

How do we do this? We cannot. *Only* the Holy Spirit of our Triune God can, as He has done numerous times in history. Including in these two great nations, far apart in Europe and in North America.

My wife Gail and I went on a fabulous trip to Scotland in the summer of 2016, with Kevin Turley's Landmark Events tours—led by American historians par excellence Bill Potter and Marshall Foster, and Scottish-born Colin Gunn (now residing in America).

We enjoyed one week in the Lowlands (flatlands) and a second week in the Highlands (mountain plains), and in countrysides, along the ocean coasts. We took a Loch Ness monster river cruise and toured small and big cities where we saw many marvelous historical sites, including the historic battlegrounds at Bothwell Bridge (and castle), numerous other battle sites, cemeteries, and many monuments. This included the William Wallace memorial, forts, and castles. Of course, we also visited the local eateries, and pretty much toured most of Scotland.

The grand tour began at the huge, historic Edinburgh Castle on the fourth of July. I wore my red-white-blue American flag shirt (as I do when home in the USA). Other tourists greeted us, including Scots and Americans wishing us a friendly Happy Independence Day as we climbed up the hill to (and from) this magnificent castle, one of many we visited. Also, we stayed on the tiny Isle of Iona where we prayed for revival and reformation in the wee hours of the Scottish morning. Then after dinner we joined the locals at the island's meeting house for their weekly folk music and dancing party. A highlight for us was when our friend Marshall Foster, wearing a swim suit in over waist-deep water on the Iona ocean shore, preached the gospel to the tour-boats ferrying to and from the historical island.

One day we visited Scottish reformer and mighty preacher John Knox's house. His preserved three-story home lies near

AT JOHN KNOX'S DESK

the Edinburgh city center area called Grass Market on the Royal Mile. Gail took a memorable picture of me there, sitting at Knox's desk, and wearing Knox's hat with his quill pen in my hand. Knox's home is just down the street from St. Giles Cathedral where he preached. Of course, we attended kirk (church) services at various cathedrals and chapels.

Gail and I picked up booklets, written by Rev. John J. Murray of Glasgow, at the Scottish Reformation Society in Edinburgh. In *Prayer for Church and Nation,* and *God Revives His Church: The Critical Importance of Revival,* Murray clearly declared mindset and plan necessary for the renewal of Scotland and the United States.

According to these booklets, *America's Great Revivals,* and Dr. Foster's *World History Institute Journal* of November 2017, history records numerous moves of God in revivals, especially over the past millennium, inspired by our loving

Creator to mankind despite our rebellion. Often Scotland appears among these great awakenings.

For example, Columba (a disciple of Saint Patrick in Ireland) went to the Isle of Iona in 553, converting much of the island. In the following century, Columba's Scottish disciples went in turn to Literariness Island in the east where, in the seventh century they converted the Anglos and Saxons in England. Later in the coming centuries, the Celtic Christians held out for true self-governing, New Testament faith against the Roman Catholic onslaught from the south. William Wallace and the Scots rose up for God and country in 1295 against the English tyrant and won their Scottish independence (for a time) in 1320 with the Declaration of Arbroath.

In the sixteenth century, John Knox and the Reformers prayed and within two decades a great Awakening swept all of Scotland into the Reformation. The Covenanters (upon signing The National Covenant of Scotland) prayed to bring another revival. Thomas Chalmers and George Whitfield once more revived the Scots at the time of the American Great Awakening of the 1740s and afterwards.

The British Isles, and especially Scotland, experienced several Holy-Spirit-led revivals in Cambusland and Kilsyth in Scotland in 1742. History reveals a tremendous parallel with American renewals, beginning with the first Great Awakening in America, a revival beginning at Northampton in 1734 and 1735, and the Second Great Awakening, ca. 1800, among others. Another Scottish revival began in 1859 (two centuries after the murder of John Brown at Priesthill). The Scots were the foremost missionaries of the 19th century.

A century later in 1947 the Hebrides Revival broke out on Lewis Island (the birth home of President Trump's mother Mary Anne MacLeod). Almost all of the 26,000 people converted on this island. The revival spread all over Scotland to Wales and England, and then to America in the 1950s through Henrietta Mears, Billy Graham, Bill Bright, Loren Cunning-

At St. Giles Cathedral

ham and other evangelists that proceeded with Holy Spirit power in dynamic ministries. The Holy Spirit has thankfully brought others in the history of the world (His Story), too.

Rev. John Murray of Glasgow proposes and we ought to consider that:

- Revival is an extraordinary work of God because it marks the abrupt reversal of an established trend and state of things among those who profess to be God's people. (Ps. 126:1)
- Revival is God restoring His work. (Hab. 3:2)
- Revival is God removing His displeasure from His people. (Ps. 85:5; 1 Cor. 11:30–32; Rev. 2:4, 14, 20; 3:19)
- Revival is God showing mercy to His church. (Hab. 3:2)

- Revival is a corporate affair. (Ps. 85:6)
- Revival is a heightening of normal Christianity. (Ps. 126:3)
- Revival is the unstopping of the pent-up energies of the Spirit of God, breaking down the dams which have been erected against His convicting and converting ministry in which communities of individuals, as happened at Pentecost and in the "awakenings" which have followed.[1]

God is a Spirit, in and of Himself infinite in being, glory, blessedness, and perfection; all-sufficient, eternal, unchangeable, incomprehensible, everywhere present, almighty, knowing all things, most wise, most holy, most just, most merciful and gracious, long-suffering, and abundant in goodness and truth. (The Westminster Larger Catechism, Answer 7)

Holy Spirit of the Living God, Fall afresh on me. Fall afresh on Scotland. Fall afresh on America.

GERALD CHRISTIAN NORDSKOG
October 31, 2017
Quincentennial of Martin Luther's 95 Theses

---

1. These points are according to Rev. John J. Murray in his aforementioned pamphlets. For the final point, Murray quotes Sinclair B. Ferguson, *The Holy Spirit: Contours of Christian Theology* (Westmont, IL: IVP Academic, 1997).

Further reading

Murray, John J. *Prayer for Church and Nation: The Nature of Earnest Prayer.* Edinburgh, U.K. and Carlisle, PA: The Banner of Truth Trust.

————. *God Revives His Church: The Critical Importance of Revival.* Edinburgh, U.K. and Carlisle, PA: The Banner of Truth Trust.

America's Great Revivals: The Story of Spiritual Revival in the United States 1734–1899. Bloomington, MN: Bethany House Publishers, 2004.

The World History Institute Journal. November/December 2017. Thousand Oaks, CA: World History Institute.

To see all of our exciting titles,
view book contents, and to get ebooks go to:
NordskogPublishing.com

If you like solid and inspiring content,
get our free **eNewsletter,**
The Bell Ringer.

We also invite you to browse the many short articles,
poems, and testimonies by various perceptive writers:
NordskogPublishing.com/category/publishers-corner/

Ask the publisher about upcoming titles,
e-books and audio versions, and a discount
when you purchase multiple books.

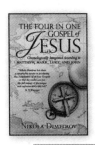

THE FOUR IN ONE GOSPEL OF JESUS:
Chronologically Integrated According to Matthew, Mark, Luke, and John

Compiled by Nikola Dimitrov

296 pp. 2017 PB $17.95

ISBN 978-0-9903774-7-4

THE BOOK THAT MADE AMERICA:
How the Bible Formed Our Nation

by Dr. Jerry Newcombe, DMin

ILLUSTRATED, INDEXED

304 pp. 2009 PB $18.95
ISBN 978-0-9824929-0-1
E-Book $11.95 Kindle $8.95
NEW: Mandarin Chinese Edition!

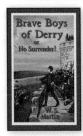

THE BRAVE BOYS OF DERRY:
No Surrender!

by W. Stanley Martin

96 pp. 2010 HB $14.95 ILLUSTRATED

ISBN 978-0-9827074-0-1

GOD'S TEN COMMANDMENTS
Yesterday, Today, Forever

by Francis Nigel Lee, LL B, D Jur, DCL, PhD, ThD

EXTENSIVE APPENDIX

128 pp. 2007 PB $11.95
E-Book 2009 $8.95 Kindle 2009 $8.95
ISBN 978-0-9796736-2-7

2716 Sailor Avenue, Ventura, CA 93001
1-805-642-2070 • 1-805-276-5129
NordskogPublishing.com